THE
TIDE
TURNS

HISTORICAL BOOKS *by*
DONALD BARR CHIDSEY

>GOODBYE TO GUNPOWDER
>
>THE BIRTH OF THE CONSTITUTION:
>*An Informal History*
>
>THE BATTLE OF NEW ORLEANS;
>*An Informal History of the War That Nobody Wanted: 1812*
>
>VALLEY FORGE
>
>JULY 4, 1776
>
>VICTORY AT YORKTOWN
>
>THE GREAT SEPARATION:
>*The Story of the Boston Tea Party and the Beginning of the American Revolution*

THE TIDE TURNS

An Informal History of the Campaign of 1776 in the American Revolution

Donald Barr Chidsey

WILDSIDE PRESS

ALSO BY THE SAME AUTHOR

NOVELS
- THE WICKEDEST PILGRIM
- RELUCTANT CAVALIER
- HIS MAJESTY'S HIGHWAYMAN
- THIS BRIGHT SWORD
- CAPTAIN BASHFUL
- LORD OF THE ISLES
- CAPTAIN ADAM
- STRONGHOLD
- PANAMA PASSAGE
- NOBODY HEARD THE SHOT
- EACH ONE WAS ALONE
- WEEPING IS FOR WOMEN
- PISTOLS IN THE MORNING

BIOGRAPHY
- ELIZABETH I
- JOHN THE GREAT:
  The Times and Life of John L. Sullivan
- THE GENTLEMAN FROM NEW YORK:
  A Biography of Roscoe Conkling
- SIR HUMPHREY GILBERT
- SIR WALTER RALEIGH
- MARLBOROUGH:
  The Portrait of a Conqueror
- BONNIE PRINCE CHARLIE

JUVENILE
- ROD RIDES HIGH

© 1966, by Donald Barr Chidsey

All pictures courtesy New York Public Library Picture Collection

CONTENTS

THE TIDE TURNS	1
NOTES	153
GLOSSARY OF EIGHTEENTH-CENTURY MILITARY TERMS	163
SELECTED BIBLIOGRAPHY	169
INDEX	179

To *Ollie Swan*

Chapter

1

CHARLES LEE was a gawky gangling stringbean of a man. He was almost unbelievably ugly, with a Cyrano's snout, small gray mocking eyes set too close together, and a smile that came and went so readily that it suggested a dose of oil—and indeed Lee could be, on occasion, oleaginous. He was eccentric almost to the point of madness. Many love dogs, but few, surely, would insist upon the company of two or three such creatures when setting out to dine with a friend or at some tavern, as Charles Lee habitually did. He was not tall, only of ordinary height, but he *seemed* tall, perhaps because of his thinness, which almost amounted to emaciation, perhaps because of the scholarly stoop of his shoulders. That stoop was much remarked upon, and with awe. In eighteenth-century America, people called a man "cultured" if he could quote a little Latin, as Lee could—and continually did. He often had in his hand a copy of Thucydides, in the original Greek. He had been everywhere, and he knew everyone. He made friends easily.

Dr. Jeremy Belknap, who met him before Boston at the time of the 1775–1776 siege, found him "a perfect original, a good scholar and soldier, and an odd genius; full of fire and passion, and but little good manners; a great sloven, wretchedly profane, and a great admirer of dogs,—of which he had two at dinner with him, one of them a native of Pomerania, which I would have taken for a bear if I had seen him in the woods."[1]

English by birth and background, Lee had only lately come to the American colonies, where he spouted many a revolutionary idea, proclaiming himself to be a belated follower of John Wilkes, Colonel Isaac Barré, and other such friends of the colonists, other such despisers of the throne. He was engaged in buying a plantation in Virginia, but though he knew many of them personally he was not in any family way connected with *the* Lees.

He was before Boston for the purpose of helping to direct the siege operations; for despite the stoop, despite too the Thucydides, this man was not a scholar, at least not a full-time scholar, but a soldier. Indeed, in the eyes of most Americans he was the soldier par excellence. He knew about the Art of War—which was customarily pronounced that way, in capitals.

There were woefully few of such on the western side of the sea. There were fighters, yes; but their fighting, excepting at the siege of Louisbourg, a conventional operation, had been done only against the redskins in frontier areas, or, in the case of the Seven Years' War, against Frenchmen who had adopted Indian methods of slaughter. In Europe it was not like that; and it was a European-type war that Great Britain was about to inflict upon its American colonies. War no longer was an individual matter, a contest waged by warriors with sword and lance. It had changed. It had become much more formal and incalculably more complicated. It was truly an art now. It was specialized, esoteric. For one thing, it had a vocabulary of its own—demilune, epaulement, flèche, redoubt, scarp, and barbette, howitzer, cohorn, abatis, saucisson—words unintelligible to the layman. It took long training to enable a man to use those terms correctly. The military mind moved in ways mysterious to the uninitiated. For instance, when the British in Boston had awakened one morning to find that the rebels were fortifying Bunker's Hill and Breed's Hill on the Charlestown peninsula across the bay, did they even consider nipping off the narrow Charlestown Neck so that supplies and reinforcements could not be thrown into the peninsula? No! That would be a direct violation of one of the fundamental rules of warfare: Never interpose a force of your own between two enemy forces. To be sure, such a move would have been easy for the crack British troops and the many British war vessels, and though it would have taken a little longer—a few days, perhaps, as compared with a few hours—it would have saved many hundreds of lives. But it would have been against the rules of the Military Art, and General Gage, supported by major generals Howe, Clinton, and Burgoyne, ordered a direct attack instead. Not just anybody would know a thing like that. It took training.

When the morning of Lexington-Concord made open conflict inevitable, the Continental Congress decided to authorize an army, and it was clear that the first thing to do after that was appoint a commander-in-chief. It was equally clear, the political situation being what it was, that this person be either a Virginian or a man from Massachusetts, for these two were the most populous and most actively patriotic of the thirteen colonies. Massachusetts had Artemas Ward and John Hancock, militia officers with no more than parade-ground experience, while Virginia had George Washington, another militiaman but one who had actually heard bullets whee past his head.[2] It may be doubted that this sound had any effect upon the decision of the Congress. The New Englanders, the despised "Wise Men of the East," had been getting things their own way in Congress for some time, and unless a conciliatory gesture were made the whole body might dissolve; so New Englanders themselves favored the naming of George Washington as commander-in-chief.

Washington, then, was appointed, and he promptly set forth to take command of the rag-tag-and-bobtail who had hemmed the British into Boston and were holding them there.

Of course Washington would need advice.

There might have been a few sour members who esteemed Charles Lee as little more than a soldier of fortune—one actually called him "a disappointed Englishman" from the floor—but most of them were dazzled by his record. He held, unquestionably, a commission as lieutenant colonel in the British Army, where the lieutenant colonels did all the field work, all the real leading—full colonelcies being but articles for sale and purchase; this commission he would have to resign before he could accept one in the American Continental Army. He had starred in Portugal. He had seen some action in the current Russo-Turkish War—but that he *had* "seen" it, a spectator rather than a participant, was not generally known. He could boast, legitimately, that he held the rank of major general in the Polish Army, and that this had been bestowed upon him by King Stanislaus, that handsome young guardsman who used Catherine of Russia's bed as a springboard to the throne; but he saw no need to add that the commission was purely and simply an honor, a title.

Lee was offered a general's commission in the Continental Army, an offer he accepted only after Congress had agreed to recompense him in the event that his inherited English fortune, estimated at £11,000, largely in land, should be confiscated as a result of this act. Thus insured—though it is hard to see how he could collect if the rebellion failed—he was appointed major general and sent to the Boston siege to help Washington, who would certainly need help.

The Tide Turns

Washington was impressed—at first. "He [Lee] is the first officer in military knowledge and experience we have in the whole Army," he wrote to his brother. "He is zealously attached to the cause, honest and well-meaning but rather fickle and violent I fear in his temper. However, as he possesses an uncommon share of good sense and spirit, I congratulate my countrymen upon his appointment to that Department."[3]

It was clear to Lee, as it was to Washington—it would be clear to anybody who glanced at a map—that the British were wasting their time in Boston and should be in New York. They were known to have sent for heavy reinforcements. Where would they put them? Boston already was overcrowded, with the comparatively small garrison there, and it depended upon ships from England for its food. A breakout could hardly result in much forage, for the countryside was up in arms. The British were in Massachusetts only because that was where the shooting had happened to start. From any sane military standpoint, New York was their town.

New York was one of the largest cities in the colonies, second only to Philadelphia, and it had the biggest and best harbor. It was an island, understandably an attraction for the world's greatest sea power. It was not fortified. It was known to be largely Tory in sentiment, and this was even more true of the rich surrounding countryside—Westchester County, northern New Jersey, Long Island.

Most important, New York controlled the mouth of the Hudson River: it controlled, that is, the southern entrance of that almost continuous waterway—the Hudson, Lake George, Lake Champlain, the Richelieu, the St. Lawrence—between New York and Quebec. Already an attempt had been made by the colonies to seal the northern end of that route by the seizure of Montreal and Quebec, but this appeared to be doomed to failure, for General Montgomery had been killed, and the second-in-command, Benedict Arnold, though fighting furiously, as always, had been beaten back. Yet even taking over all of Canada would not in itself have been enough; for if the British could control the sail-navigable portion of the Hudson, say as far north as Albany, they would effectively cut all communications (for they were in complete command of the sea) between New England and the middle and southern colonies, which meant that they would strangle the revolution. *Ergo:* New York was their dish.

Washington wanted Lee to go to New York, raise the militia in that state and in Connecticut and New Jersey, and study the port facilities and the possibility of fortifying the place. Lee wanted very much to do this. Congress, politically conscious, procrastinated. Washington was called commander-in-chief, but he did not know whether he had the authority to make such an appointment, to give such a sweeping order. He did not know where he stood with the Continental Congress. Nobody ever did. He asked John Adams, who was in Quincy to see Abigail during a Congressional recess, and Adams told him, sure, go ahead. So Washington did, January 8, 1776, being careful to write into the order that Lee should execute his plan "keeping always in view the declared intentions of Congress"—whatever they were.

Lee arrived on the scene February 4. He must have been dismayed by what he met. This was not his first visit to New York—he got around a good bit—but it was the first time he had been called upon to appraise the chances of that place holding off an invader: he saw right away that those chances were not good. A more vulnerable spot it would be hard to conceive. Here was an island thirteen miles long and between one and two miles wide, an island running north and south and easily approached from the sea, the south. Its population of about 25,000 was largely clustered in some 4,000 buildings in the southern three miles, most of them in the very bottom mile: the rest, where it was not open wilderness, was farm land. The contemptible Bronx River formed a northern boundary, but the rest was wide open. The Hudson River, a major stream, stretched along the west; the East River stretched along the east. Each of these was navigable by vessels of the deepest draft. There were few hills on the island, none at all in the southern part. There were no natural defensive positions. The city *asked* to be seized.

In addition to this, most of the merchants as well as many if not most of the farmers held strong loyalist views and would, it could be assumed, cooperate with any landing attempt.

Not all of the American colonists favored separation from the mother country. It had been estimated that about one-third was for independence and one-third was strongly against it; the third third just didn't care.

Charles Lee, after studying it, did not say that the island could be successfully defended. He did, however, come up with a plan calculated to make it very hard to get, very expensive. He would place a row of cannons at the southern tip (a district to this day called the Battery) and fortify nearby Governor's Island. He would build a large fort on heights overlooking the Hudson, far up in the northern part of the island, and a corresponding fort opposite this on the New Jersey shore, the object of these being to keep war vessels and transports from sailing up as far as Westchester County and turning the garrison's flank. He laid out a series of redoubts and batteries along the East River. None of this would do any good if an invader could first take Brooklyn Heights, as Lee's professional eye told him. Most of Long Island was flat farm land, though at the western end, where the village of Brooklyn faced lower Manhattan, the settlement served by the Wall Street ferry, there were many marshes (the name itself comes from the Dutch *Breukelen*, "marshy land"). Behind this village was an arched row of hills from the top of which cannon could control the whole lower end of New York island, so narrow was the East River at this point. Those heights must on no account be left without protection, Charles Lee decreed.

The first thing to do, of course, was to make things so disagreeable for the local loyalists that they would leave town in droves, making room for the militiamen who would erect all those fortifications. This Lee did, with the enthusiastic assistance of the local Whigs. It was the logical thing to do, in a civil war.

But he never really did get a chance to implement his plan, for he was summoned elsewhere to met another crisis.

Major General Henry Clinton sailed out of Boston Bay with a large fleet, and it was feared at first that he might have designs upon New York, as Lee was promptly notified. Spies along the shore, however, reported him to be heading south, and the Continental high command guessed (correctly) that he meant to hit Charleston, South Carolina. The loss of that key port would endanger the whole of the South, where there was a great deal of loyalist feeling, so General Lee was called off the New York assignment and hurried south, with orders to teach the Carolinians how to defend themselves. He left March 7.

On March 17—there were very few Irish in Boston then, and nobody remarked that it was Saint Patrick's Day—Howe pulled out. Ever since Henry Knox had hauled the cannons from Ticonderoga and Crown Point, enabling Washington to fortify Dorchester Heights, it had been obvious that Howe would have to go. He took his time, warning Washington, though not in public, that he would burn the city if those guns spoke. He had a lot to move—the recently reinforced navy contingent, his own soldiers, and many hundreds of loyalist sympathizers who did not dare to remain behind.

With this huge, this ponderous, fleet he at last moved out to the open sea. There he paused for several days, while those ashore wondered why. Washington in particular was on pins and needles. He was eager to go to New York and supervise the completion of the Lee plan, but he could not venture to leave Boston until he had seen which way Howe's fleet turned. *It* might constitute the descent upon New York.

At last Howe did move—north, toward Halifax.

But he would be back! Oh, assuredly he would be back!

Washington sped to New York, where he arrived April 13. There were weeks and even months of work, dull work, mostly digging—but it had to be done. There was a great deal of sickness in camp, where the turnover was bewildering and desertion a daily problem. The news from the North was bad, and there was, ominously, no news at all from the South. Continental outposts on Long Island, on Sandy Hook, every day scanned the horizon in vain for warships, for transports.

It was not until June 25 that the British began to come; but once they had started coming it did seem as though they would never stop.

Chapter 2

When Queen Anne died, in 1714, the nearest Protestant heir to the throne of Great Britain and Ireland, the fat Elector of Hanover, consented to rule as George I. He knew not a word of English, but this did not matter, for he brought his court with him. In this court were two of his mistresses (his wife, years earlier, had been locked in a remote *schloss* for having made eyes at an adventurous count) who had charge of all patronage and whose fingers were exceedingly sticky. These ladies were the Baroness von Kielmannsegge and the Baroness von Schulenberg, though the English public usually called them, because of their respective figures, "the Elephant" and "the Beanpole." Quite openly they sold offices and titles, and since they were avaricious they were not popular. Once their coach was stopped by a London near-mob, which muttered ominously. Von Kielmannsegge (the Elephant) leaned out of a window and appealed to them in broken English: "We have yust come here for all your goods!" "Yes, damn you," somebody shouted back, "and for all our chattels too!"

The Howe brothers were rumored to be the grandsons

of George I and the Baroness von Kielmannsegge, who had been created Countess of Darlington in the English peerage. If true, it is not to be wondered at that their careers took on an early brightness, each destined to be distinguished.

George Augustus, the oldest, had inherited the Irish title of Viscount Howe. He was an ardent soldier, an ardent friend too of the colonists, whom he liked and who liked him. When he was killed before Ticonderoga, in 1758, every good American knew that a friend had been lost. The people of Massachusetts, in whose name he had fought, raised money by popular subscription to erect a monument to him in Westminster Abbey.

The title descended to the second son, Richard, a navy man, a reserved personage known to those under him as "Black Dick," not because of his moodiness but because of his complexion and his bushy sable eyebrows (his hair of course was powdered).

The third and last was William. He too was dark complexioned. He was a good-natured, easy-going man. He had poor teeth. His life was the army, and he probably would have risen to a major generalship even if he had not happened to be a cousin of the King. He had covered himself with glory at Quebec. He had written a book on infantry tactics. It was he who had led the attacking forces at Breed's Hill, where he had been splashed in blood to the thighs while every one of his aides was hit, though he himself miraculously escaped unwounded. Breed's Hill—that is, the battle for Bunker Hill[4]—had made a profound impression upon General Howe. Sure, death was his business; but you did not have to have *that* much death all at one time. Soldiers were expensive. There must have been something better than a simple frontal attack. He was a great believer in flanking movements.

General Howe arrived in lower New York Bay aboard *Greyhound* and in the company of two other warships, the

GENERAL WILLIAM HOWE

The Tide Turns 13

advance guard, the harbinger. They dropped hooks, and waited. Four days later, June 29, no fewer than forty-five vessels put in, and the day after *that* there were eighty-two arrivals, and the disembarkation of troops on Staten Island began. These had come from Halifax.

There was no opposition. Staten Island had been cleared of Whigs and all their livestock well in advance, and the meat-hungry troopers, after those weary weeks at sea, were not overly kind even to the Tories who remained. Tents went up everywhere. Drums were rolled, orders barked, drills held. O-mouthed men on the New Jersey shore, peering through spyglasses, never had seen anything like this before. Nobody in America had. This was not a few skimpy regiments, a thousand or so redcoats.[5] This was an army.

July 4 the Continental Congress at Philadelphia, unintimidated, adopted the Declaration of Independence. Headquarters in New York was officially informed of this fact on the 9th, and Washington gave orders that at evening parade it should be read before each individual company. So it was that thousands heard for the first time Jefferson's stirring words: "When in the course of human events . . ." Afterward there was a great deal of cheering, and a large crowd of civilians, aided perhaps by a few soldiers—you could not tell the difference, since there were no uniforms—descended upon the heroic equestrian statue of King George III in the Bowling Green. The statue depicted the monarch in an unbecoming Roman toga. It had been cast in lead and gilded on the outside, and it stood on a white marble pedestal eighteen feet high. The crowd got ropes around it, and they heaved with a will, and they toppled the thing to the ground, where they chopped it into large chunks to be sent to a Connecticut factory and molded into cannonballs and musket balls for the Continental Army. After that everybody cheered again, and they scattered for yet another drink.

General Howe, in his camp on Staten Island, heard of the Declaration of Independence with dismay. It might have meant that he came too late.

The Howe family tradition of sympathy for the American cause was a whit condescending, but sincere. When he had stood for Parliament, a few years earlier, General Howe had promised his constituents that he would never, on any account, make war upon their and his cousins—uncouth cousins to be sure, but cousins all the same—in America. After he had accepted the command his excuse was: "I was given orders—I had no choice." Now he was troubled. The colonists had pronounced themselves independent even before he and his brother Richard—who was expected off Sandy Hook any day now—could approach them with His Gracious Majesty's gracious offer of conciliation and, in certain laid-down circumstances, pardon.

For the Howes had been designated to be not merely a scourge but a dove of peace. It was the old carrot-and-stick game. They were to purr and to growl alternately, or, if they could possibly manage this, simultaneously. They were to flex the royal biceps and shake the royal fist, but at the same time wink with a knowing smile and whisper soft let's-get-togethers.

William did nothing about his secret orders just then. He was waiting for Richard.

Richard came a few days later, the 12th, and under his command, direct from England, were no fewer than 150 warships of the line, frigates, tenders, schooners, sloops, bomb ketches, and transports, especially transports, many of which bore designations allusive of one-half of the Admiral's mission—*Friendship, Good Intent, Amity's Admonition, Felicity*, and the like.[6] The goggle-eyed watchers at the Battery could not at that distance make out the individual figures of soldiers and sailors, but they could and did see the masts, a forest.

ADMIRAL RICHARD HOWE

Richard, even before he went ashore, sat down and wrote a letter to his old friend and chess opponent Benjamin Franklin, until recently representative in London of several American colonies, now a delegate to the Continental Congress. Black Dick proposed, in effect, that they have a little talk about the possibility of peace. Franklin's answer was prompt enough, and it was properly polite, but it was stiff and noncommittal, which was not like him.

The Brothers Howe then framed a declaration addressed to the American people. It was resoundingly vague. It promised pardons, but did not say how many or under what conditions. It did not even mention independence, treating the Congressional action of July 4 as though it had never happened, or, at best, had been an egregious mistake, about which the less said the better.

A copy of this declaration, together with a letter couched "in the most genteel terms possible," was put into a packet addressed to "George Washington, Esq., etc., etc., etc.," and sent to New York under a flag of truce.

The young lieutenant who bore this missive was met at the Battery by two colonels, sharp-eyed Joseph Reed, Washington's adjutant general, and roly-poly bull-voiced Henry Knox, his chief of artillery, who until lately had been, respectively, a Philadelphia lawyer and a Boston bookseller. They were togged out as became the occasion—epaulettes, dress swords, and the pink chest ribbons and black cockades of members of the general staff. The lieutenant, who might have been expecting something Neanderthaloid, was impressed.

The lieutenant, however, was dashed when, after having glanced at the superscription, Knox and Reed shook their heads. They knew nobody by that name, they said. They knew General George Washington, Commander-in-Chief of the Continental Army of America, but no "George Washington, Esq., etc., etc., etc." They sent the letter back.

A little later, in the house Knox was using as his headquarters, the Kennedy House, a short distance up Broadway on the west side, the colonels reported to Washington, who thanked them for carrying out his orders. Washington then wrote an account of the incident to Congress, protesting that he would never let his own dignity get between the American people and their welfare, but that he had been thinking of the dignity of Congress. Washington was always careful in his treatment of Congress. In this instance he was thanked.

The Howes tried again a few days later, this time sending Lieutenant Colonel Paterson, a staff officer, William Howe's own adjutant general.

Patterson asked for and was granted an audience with George Washington himself. Paterson's eyes were not blindfolded, as was the military custom for the bearer of a white flag, and he solemnly thanked Knox and Reed, and later Washington, for this indulgence.

In the Kennedy House, Paterson explained to Washington that the "etc., etc., etc." of the previous epistle was not meant as any sort of slur: it was only meant to cover whatever titles Washington might have. In that event, Washington replied, it did not mean anything.

Paterson set forth the nature of the Howes' peace commission and said that the brothers hoped very much that there might be an accommodation. Urbane, but firm, Washington stopped him. He lacked the authority, Washington said, to discuss peace. Anything like that would have to be taken up with the Continental Congress; and he called for wine, closing the conversation.

Paterson was astounded. Why, the fellow was a gentleman!

In the doorway he turned for one last try. Was there not any message General Washington would like to give to Admiral and General Howe?

"Only my compliments," was the reply.

And that was that—for the present.

On the very day of Black Dick's arrival, two British frigates, *Phoenix*, 44, and *Rose*, 28, together with the schooner-of-war *Tryal*, and two tenders, sailed out of the lower bay and up the Hudson past Fort Washington on the east shore and Fort Constitution on the west, past all the shore batteries situated above and below these, past the sundry sunken ships, and cables, and underwater chevaux-de-frise. The frigates fired as they went, and they were unscathed. Not only were the shore batteries ineffective but in some cases the gun handlers, frightened, under fire for the first time, ran away. The only casualties were on the American side—six killed when a mishandled cannon exploded. The *Phoenix* and the *Rose* and their attendants sailed up the river for about forty miles, to the Tappan Zee, and there they anchored for a few days, after which they sailed back in leisurely fashion, again sneering at everything the Continental guns could throw. It was very disheartening.

Still the fleet in the lower bay and the army on Staten Island did not budge. There was no movement of vessels, so close together that a jolly boat could scarcely wind its way among them, and every morning and every night a thousand wobbling columns of smoke rose from the island, where the farmers were finding that their rail fences disappeared like snow upon the desert's dusty face; but though there were foraging parties, there was no massed movement. What in the world were they waiting for, down there? *More* reinforcements?

The only good news came from the South, where a fleet under Sir Peter Parker and carrying an army under Clinton had ingloriously failed to take Charleston. In the eyes of Carolinians, who were there, this beating-off, a clear-cut patriots' victory, had been due to their own militia general, William

Moultrie. In the eyes of Charles Lee it had been due to Charles Lee. He had occupied the Governor's House while in Charleston, where he passed out a great deal of polysyllabic advice. He was on his way back to New York now, bowing to right and left, airily accepting ceremonial swords and testimonial scrolls, a hero. There were those in Manhattan who muttered that it was as well that he was returning, that it was about time the Continental cause had somebody who knew how to run an army.

The visible evidence of the Charleston victory showed up in lower New York Bay, and it still looked mighty fit. Parker's 9 warships and Clinton's 30 transports had been mauled a bit, but they had not been smashed. They were as good as ever.

Still nothing happened.

On August 12 there arrived from Europe Commodore Hotham and 6 warships escorting 28 transports jam packed with 2,600 guardsmen and 8,000 German mercenaries.

This was possibly the greatest military-naval host yet assembled anywhere. It was by far the greatest ever sent forth by Great Britain. There were 427 vessels in all, 52 of them warships. There were 10,000 sailors and 32,000 soldiers, headed by 6 generals. The whole show had cost £850,000 so far. By any standard of comparison—tonnage, men, guns, vessels—it was more than twice as big as the Spanish Armada.

Even then, even after the arrival of the Hessians and the guardsmen, ten more days of some of the finest campaign weather on record were allowed to pass before the Howe brothers made their move.

Chapter 3

THE BOATS had been built especially for this occasion. They were flatboats, 75 of them—slow, clumsy, shallow-draft vessels capable of holding many men provided that there was no sea running. There were also 11 batteaux for carrying cannon. Soldiers could wade, but fieldpieces could not; so that each batteau had a square-ended bow that could be dropped on chains to form a ramp or gangplank to the shore, a device by no means new to military movement but assuredly a novelty in America. In and out among them, like gigantic water bugs, skittered a couple of supervisory galleys.

A frigate, *Rainbow*, loafed off Denyse Point, the westernmost tip of Long Island, the Long Island side of the Narrows. Three other frigates and a couple of bomb ketches were anchored in Gravesend Bay, a few miles east of Denyse Point on the south shore of Long Island: they would cover the landing.

The main British camp on Staten Island was situated right near the Narrows, and it was from that point, at eight o'clock on the morning of August 22, that the boats began to appear. It must have been a glorious sight, and even a stately one, despite a lack of grace on the part of the boats themselves. The day was drenched with sunlight, and this shone upon the scarlet coats, the pipe-clayed crossbelts, the golden gorgets that the officers wore, the impeccably serried muskets, the flags, the regimental colors. Here was storybook warfare, real storybook warfare, the best kind.

There was no resistance. The only persons to greet these invaders on the beach at Gravesend Bay were local farmers, who hoped to sell them produce. The British and the Hessians were not paid much, and what little they might have been entitled to was tied up in various routine withholding funds for maintenance and the like—for even a couple of coins in pocket would be a temptation to desert—and they had no intention of exchanging cash for goods. Instead, they went to work among the apple orchards, of which there were many in that vicinity. As gay as schoolboys on a picnic, they had soon stripped every tree.

The boats, expertly handled by seamen from the fleet, went back to Staten Island. The first load had been 4,000 men. The second was larger—5,000. By noon all had been disembarked, and the sun still shone.

The landing did not go unwatched. Brooklyn Heights had for some time been occupied by the Continentals.

Brooklyn Heights was not really very high, about one hundred feet above the surface of the East River, but its importance as a place from which artillery could command all of New York town had been recognized not only by Lee but by each general who subsequently had sought to implement Lee's preliminary plan. The "Heights" were low hills, thickly wooded, pierced in only three places by roads—the Flatbush road, nearest to the sea, the Bedford road, and, on the Continental extreme left, the Jamaica road. The first two were heavily guarded—though not heavily enough for the massive power that Howe seemed about to throw against them. The

Jamaica road was not guarded, and indeed was not even patrolled.

There was also another way of getting from the Flatbush plain to the fortifications along the East River, and this was the so-called Gowanus road, which was not, properly, a pass, for it did not pierce but rounded the Heights. This formed the American right.

The American line was roughly an arc. The right was protected by Gowanus Creek and the marshes there. The center was protected by a great deal of infantry and even a few small fieldpieces. The left—no one, now, will ever know why—was left "up in the air."

Behind these natural defenses the Americans had built a line of trenches, redoubts, and small forts, pinching off a peninsula of about a mile and a half width, between Gowanus Bay and Wallabout Bay. This could be occupied by a falling-back movement if the passes through the Heights were forced; and in that position, attacked from the interior of Long Island, it was undoubtedly strong; but if British warships ever got up the East River it could be hammered to bits from, as it were, behind. A battery of small and rusty guns along the shore and along the opposite shore of New York, and also four guns emplaced at Red Hook, the westernmost tip of the fortified line, facing out over Buttermilk Channel, were expected to keep the British Navy away. What did keep that navy away was a stiff wind from the northeast, though ordinarily in August the prevailing wind was from the southwest. The shore guns were only a fond hope. They could never have survived a slam-bang fight with warships.

Washington knew that the position could not be defended for long, but he knew too that Congress wanted it defended as long as possible. Morale demanded as much.

But he had been misinformed. He thought that there were only a few thousand British on Long Island, and he assumed that this would be no more than a diversion, and that the real attack would be launched against Manhattan itself, directly. Therefore he stayed at his headquarters, the Morris House, on that island.[7]

He assumed, too, that the British would strike right away, right after landing, as he himself would have done. He did not know Howe, a man who always took his time. The British put up tents, and they strayed farther afield in search of more orchards. There was a little skirmishing in the passes, a faint feeling-out, but it did not amount to anything.

On the 25th the warships took their stations again and the flatboats were put back into service when General von Heister was ferried over from Staten Island to Gravesend Bay with two whole brigades of mercenaries. These men occupied the original Flatbush camp of the British. The earlier Hessians and the Black Watch Highlanders were in the center, a camp at Flatlands that covered the Bedford pass. The rest of the army, which included some of the crack light-infantry regiments and was led by no fewer than four generals—Percy, Clinton, Cornwallis, and Howe himself—was moved to the extreme British right.

This development, made on a flat plain in broad daylight, necessarily was witnessed by hundreds of Americans, yet nobody seems to have drawn the conclusion that Howe was planning to deliver a hard right hook. The Jamaica pass remained unpatrolled.

Washington crossed to Long Island, looked over the array, conferred with generals Putnam and Sullivan, and went back to Manhattan. He saw that the Long Island push was to be a bigger one than he had at first been led to expect, and he did send over some small but good reinforcements; but he still kept more than two-thirds of his army in New York.

A skilled intelligence service could have warned him about that suspicious troop-shifting; but he had no intelli-

THE BRITISH FLEET IN LOWER NEW YORK BAY DURING THE BATTLE OF LONG ISLAND

gence of any sort at this time. Cavalry could at least have scouted that exposed wing; but there was no cavalry.

Perhaps if Nathanael Greene had not come down with a fever the story might have been different.

The lot of a surgeon in the British Army was not a happy one. He was paid six shillings a day, but so much of this was withheld for subsistence that in fact he got little more than a private. He was expected to furnish his own instruments, and in some cases his own medicines. At least he did not have to bring in the wounded: that was the responsibility of their friends in the field. So a surgeon seldom was shot. But he had no dignity, no status. He was merely a sawbones. He did not mess with the officers, and he rated no salute, not even a "sir." With a whole regiment to take care of, he might or might not have a surgeon's mate assigned to him, and the "mate" was customarily a man the colonel could not think of any other place for. Neither of these miserable wretches was required to be a physician or to have any sort of medical experience at all. "Surgeon" was a courtesy title.

In the Continental Army it was even worse. In the beginning nobody on the American side had expected a long war, so that supplies were limited and no means of replenishing them were provided. There were shortages of everything, and gravest of all was the shortage of doctors. There were not enough of these to go around even in civilian life, and while one might take to the field as a patriotic gesture if there happened to be an action nearby, he could hardly be expected to travel from place to place with the army, leaving his own patients at home unattended.

The result, sanitary conditions being what they were, was a great deal of sickness. At any given time as much as 30 percent of Washington's army might be on hospital call. It was a major problem, but nothing much was done about it. It was a problem in transportation too, when the army was on the move: to leave your wounded and sick behind you was inhumane.

Smallpox had chewed huge chunks out of the Army of the North, so that this army could not hold the gains it had made. Not smallpox but a somewhat mysterious ailment known as "camp fever" was to plague Washington's army in New York that summer, laying up men by the score, by the hundreds. It wasn't fatal, but it was damned uncomfortable, and to ignore it only meant to make it worse. When Nathanael Greene came down with "camp fever," just a few days before the British moved in on Long Island, he quite rightly took to his bed.

A blacksmith is supposed to be burly. Greene was not. A self-taught Rhode Islander, he had reasonably broad shoulders; but he was short, and nobody could dub him, despite his calling, brawny. He had suffered all his life from arthritis, which had permanently affected his left knee, so that he limped, a most unsoldierly gait. Yet soldiering fascinated him, and he had gulped down everything about military tactics that he could lay hands on. He had been read out of the Society of Friends because of this un-Quakerish attitude. He was what sports writers would call a "natural." He made mistakes, but not many of them. His snap judgments tended to be more sound than the methodically reasoned decisions of any council of war. He had an instinct for fights.

Greene had been in command of the installations and troops on Long Island, and he was of course familiar with every foot of the territory. When he was obliged to report sick, his post was assigned to John Sullivan, a New Hampshire lawyer, ambitious, industrious, reliable, but no great shakes as a general, nothing to be compared with Nathanael Greene. Sullivan never had a chance to examine the terrain closely. He in turn was superseded at the last moment by Israel ("Old Put") Putnam, the French and Indian War hero from Connecticut, a person colorful, to be sure, a person downright *scintillant*, but one with no experience in fieldwork such as this.

There were other involuntary absentees. The only two regiments in the Continental Army at this time that could by any stretch of imagination be described as "smart" or "crack" were Smallwood's Marylanders and Haslet's Delawareans. These were made up of young men of good families, filled with ardor for the patriot cause, and they wore uniforms, a rare thing in that rabble. They were well disciplined, had worked hard, and could be depended upon. They were sent across the East River at the last moment and were stationed inside of the fortified lines near the river, to be thrown in as reinforcements where needed. Each was under the command of its major only, both of the colonels and both of the lieutenant colonels being detained on Manhattan to serve with a court-martial, which apparently was esteemed more important than the impending battle.

This was the situation when on the night of August 26 General Howe unleashed his right hook. It was to prove lethal.

Chapter

4

THE WAR was not popular in Britain, and recruitment limped. Ireland ordinarily was a fertile field, but it happened that there was no famine in Ireland at the moment, so that the sergeants beat their drums in vain, for who wanted to enlist when there were plenty of potatoes? Scotland, and especially the Highlands—so poor as a result of stern post-Culloden legislation—contributed a few husky lads, but not nearly enough. In England itself the jails were scraped as usual, and the gin mills, the gutters, the brothels; but the take was tiny.

Recourse was had, then, to Catherine II, Empress of Russia. At first this might seem startling. Catherine, a correspondent of Voltaire, not without some reason rated herself as the most enlightened monarch in Europe. Yet she came from a small German state, Anhalt-Zerbst, where her brother the prince was a leading huckster in soldiery. Catherine, for all her professed liberality, was quite prepared to charter a 20,-000-man Russian army to Great Britain if the price was right. The deal fell through not because of any scruples on her part but because her neighbor and mentor, Frederick of Prussia, Frederick the Great, said "no"; and Frederick's "no," the situation being what it was, was decisive. The King of Prussia, though surely no pacifistic milksop, differed from most of the German princes of his time in that he thought that the buying and selling of cannon fodder was a dirty, degrading business; and he didn't mind saying so.

So Britain turned with a sigh to those Teutonic noblemen whose principalities produced rigidly disciplined regiments and those alone. Past experience had proved that these landgraves and margraves and dukes and princes, always desperately in debt, drove hard bargains; and so it was again. In a series of contracts—each was in the form of a separate treaty between Great Britain and an independent German state, but for all intents and purposes they were common business contracts—the country that sought to crush its revolting colonists agreed to pay so-and-so-much (the prices varied widely) for so-and-so-many soldiers. The biggest dealers were the Landgrave of Hesse-Cassel and his son, William, Count of Hesse-Hanau, so that all of the soldiers supplied came to be called Hessians, though they hailed as well from Brunswick-Luneberg, Anspach-Bayreuth, Waldeck, and Anhalt-Zerbst. The whole package would come close to 30,000 men. Not all of these were to be paid over immediately, though most were—others being replacements. Not all were slated for direct service in America, where it was planned to keep only about 20,000 at a given time; the rest were to be told off for guard duty at imperial outposts such as Gibraltar, where they would relieve regular British Army units, which could then be sent to quell the Americans.

Hessians fell into three classes. As much can be said for the members of most armies, true, but the class lines were much more sternly maintained in the case of the Hessians.

The officers were all aristocrats. In the British Army, an ambitious commoner might squeeze in now and then, for commissions had prices attached to them, and a rich merchant's son, say, provided that he was at least literate and did not look and act like a pig strayed from some sty, with only a modicum of political pull could buy himself into the ranks of the British officers, though he could not pick his regiment. It was not so on the Continent, where you had to have a title in order to qualify for a commission.[8] Such personages, of course, had inelastic ideas about the duty of a subject to his prince. Disloyalty to the God-assigned monarch, in their eyes, was the most appalling of all sins. It was as bad as desertion, which, when you came to think of it, *was* a form of disloyalty. The American rebels, then, could be and should be treated as wild animals.

The second class was made up of the sergeants—tough, efficient men, full-time professionals. It was they who did the recruiting: they would do anything for pay. It was they who enforced the strictest discipline in the world by means of the harshest punishments in the world.

Of the rank and file there might be here and there a townsman, but the great majority were of the soil. They were peasants in the full, flat, eighteenth-century meaning of that word. They did what they were told, and did it in silence. On paper, only a few of them were conscripted; the rest had volunteered. But they were what Central Americans would call *voluntarios forçados*. If they *hadn't* volunteered when told to, they would have been hit on the head and shanghaied.

This same meek-mannered bovine creature was soon transformed into an ogre. His towering hat (meant, like his high-heeled boots, to make him look even taller than he was) was fronted with brass. His knee-high gaiters were black. His musket was very long, very heavy; and he carried, besides a heavy and long bayonet, a brass-hilted sword. In a clean-shaven age he was encouraged to grow a long, bushy, fiercely curled mustache, which he dyed with the same blacking he used on his boots. His queue of artificial hair, pasted with flour, hung down his back as far as the waist; and this too, like the mustaches—it is hard to see why—was calculated to strike terror into the beholder.

The wildest stories about these monsters were circulated in the Continental camps. The Hessians were said to be taught to kill blindly, right and left, without any heed of cries for mercy; they were said deliberately to ignore surrender attempts.

For their part, the Hessians no doubt were uneasy as they went into battle on Long Island the night of August 26–27, 1776. They were sure to fight fiercely, for they did not dare to stall or to run away, so terrible were the punishments, and they had been taught that above all they should never permit themselves to be captured, for they were assured —and probably most of them believed it—that the Americans ate their prisoners.

Not Germans but a couple of flamboyant Scots were the first to tangle on Long Island. Major General Sir James Grant, of Ballendallock, was an enormously fat aristocrat who had fought with distinction in the French and Indian War and who entertained an extremely low opinion of Americans as soldiers. "Give me five thousand troops," he had boasted in Parliament, "and I'll march from one end of the colonies to the other." He had just about 5,000 men under him when a little after three o'clock on the morning of the 27th he started to drive in the outposts of the American right wing in the Gowanus Bay sector. Israel Putman, awakened, sent the Marylanders and the Delawareans in as reinforcements, but even then the Continental commander in that area, Brigadier General Stirling, had a bare 1,600 men, most of whom had never before been under fire.

William Alexander always styled himself "Lord Stirling." He signed his letters simply "Stirling," and was "my lord"-ed by all friends and acquaintances. The son of a staunch Jacobite, he had settled in Basking Ridge, New Jersey, where he lived in style—a plump, rufous, jovial man who liked his liquor. His troops adored him.

In 1759 this exuberant Scot had gone back to Britain for an expensive attempt to have his title, the Earl of Stirling, validated: it had lapsed. A jury granted the award, but the House of Lords disallowed the grant, and officially, on the records, William Alexander remained exactly that—William Alexander. To his friends, however, he was Lord Stirling.

As it happened, he had heard General Grant make that monumental boast in the House of Commons. In England at the time, in search of his ancestors' elusive title, he had been in the visitors' gallery. He told the troops of this, that morning on Long Island.

Stirling may not have been much of a strategist but he was a first-class fighting man. He might have beaten a slow, steady retreat. He had men he could not rely on. He was faced with a large force of regulars. His rear was threatened, for five of Admiral Howe's vessels were struggling against that stiff north wind to get into Buttermilk Channel, and if they ever succeeded they could cut his thin force to pieces in a matter of minutes. But Stirling elected to stand his ground. He had no orders, and it probably never even occurred to him to run away. He drew his men up in battle array.

The British came to a point about five hundred yards away, where they ground to a stop. When the light allowed, they sent forward some infantry troops who occupied an orchard about one hundred yards from the Continental front line, and from there they began to bang away with their muskets, a fire the Americans promptly returned. Why did they waste powder and ball at such a distance? The Americans found it unsettling to be fired on without firing back, and they wished to show that they were not afraid. But the

LORD STIRLING AT THE BATTLE OF LONG ISLAND

British veterans? They were only obeying orders. Grant was not supposed to attack—not yet. He was only supposed to make a big brave show.

After a while the light infantry fell back, away from the orchard, and joined the main body of British troops. Then the guns opened up—two three-pounders on the part of the Americans, a couple of heavy howitzers on the part of the British. They made a great deal of noise, but they did scarcely any more damage than the muskets had done.

One of Howe's warships, *Roebuck*, did get close enough to the battery at Red Hook to exchange a few inconclusive shots with it, but soon it had to fall back. The others were and would remain well out of range.

The Americans, though they expected to be charged at any moment, stayed firm. *They* did not know that this was only a feint. Especially when Grant sent back for reinforcements—the 42nd Highlanders and a couple of companies of loyalists—did it look as though an attack would come soon.

The war already was a year and a half old, but this was the first time that Americans had stood up to British regulars in the open field, without cover.

In the center, at first, the combat was equally inconclusive. There General von Heister, leading his own Hessians and the Highlanders of the Black Watch, also had orders to make a lot of noise but not to press too hard. There was a great deal of cannonading, and the Americans in the Bedford pass and the Flatbush pass felt their stomachs wamble as they looked down on a sea of bare bright bayonets; but nothing much happened—until about nine o'clock, when all hell broke loose.

That was when the British right wing opened up—*behind* the American lines.

They had been marching all night, 10,000 troops, some of the best in the world, and they carried with them twenty-eight pieces of artillery. The van was commanded by Clinton, and behind him came Cornwallis, Percy, and Howe, in that order. This column was almost two miles long. It had formed and started, guided by three local Tories, as soon as darkness permitted, about nine o'clock.

A halt was made at midnight in order to give the men a short rest, and at that time an advance party came in with five young Continental officers, mounted men, whom they had surprised and captured. These young men had been sent out by General Sullivan, who paid them out of his own pocket to keep an eye on the Jamaica pass. Five men! Questioned by Cornwallis and Clinton, they declared that the pass was unguarded. This was simply too good to be true in the eyes of the British generals, who had expected to fight their way through, and when the column resumed its march it did so with great caution, light-infantry outfits thrown out ahead. But, sure enough, the pass was wholly unguarded; and they marched right through.

They swung west, toward the rear of the American lines. They showed no light and they made no sound. When, as occasionally happened, it was necessary to remove some small trees to get the guns past, these were sawed rather than chopped down, for the sake of silence.

It was a masterpeice of manoeuvring. It was brilliant. They were lucky, true; but they were superb.

When daylight came they were extra careful to raise no dust. It would be a hot clear day. Their bayonets were not fixed but scabbarded by their sides, lest they reflect the sun.

A colonel of Pennsylvania riflemen, Samuel Miles, who was serving under General Sullivan near the Bedford pass, at about seven o'clock that morning took it into his head to march his 400-odd men to the extreme left end of the line and see if the Jamaica pass was all right. Seemingly he did this without any order or any sort of authorization, and possibly without even giving notice. Colonels in the Continental Army were independent commanders, at least in their own eyes. This was just an idea that Miles had.

The Pennsylvanians for a while, then, were marching east, while less than half a mile away the British were marching west. Neither column saw or heard the other. At about eight o'clock, when Miles and his men did stumble upon the British column, it was not the van—that was several miles to their rear—but the baggage train they met. This was well guarded, and the British attacked promptly. Heavily outnumbered, the Pennsylvanians broke and ran. About half of them were captured. The others gained the East River line of fortifications—temporary safety.

The sound of musketry and rifle fire from the rear and to

THE RETREAT ACROSS GOWANUS CREEK

the left must have disconcerted the Americans posted in the passes; but everything was a little mixed up that morning.

At nine o'clock, in the little village of Bedford, the British fired two heavy cannons.

That was the signal. It was then that the Hessians and the Black Watch ceased to do parade-ground movements and drove in—with bayonets.

The Americans were trapped, assailed from front and rear at the same time. Some of them surrendered on the spot. Most of them dove into the woods and tried to make their way to the East River lines. Many were shot down as they ran: most of the American casualties of the day occurred here. Others were captured. Still others—in small, breathless, scared groups—made it.

One of those who surrendered was General Sullivan himself.

Grant did not launch his attack as soon as he heard the signal. The truth is, what with all his sham fighting he had let himself get dangerously low on ammunition, and he had sent out to the flagship of the fleet to ask for more. Admiral Howe not only sent him powder and cartridges but also 2,000 Marines he hadn't expected. When he got those Marines into battle formation, Grant attacked.

Stirling's command was magnificent. It did not panic. It had no orders; there was no chance for reinforcements, for Cornwallis's brigade, the second in the British flanking movement, had not paused to participate in the action at the Bedford and Flushing passes but had swept on to complete the encompassment, and it was now blocking the Gowanus road, posted in enormous numbers between Stirling and the fortifications.

Four times the Continentals tried to fight their way through, and four times they were thrown back. Then they did the only thing left to them, short of surrender. They slopped across the marches and into Gowanus Creek. There some waded, the water up to their necks, while others swam. Grape and canister and musket balls were whitening the water all around them, and some, of course, never did make it; but many did.

Stirling himself got lost in the excitement and found himself in the midst of a lot of Hessians. He surrendered his sword to General von Heister.

Two major generals in one day was a good bag. There were 900-odd other prisoners, besides American casualties of some 500. The total British casualties were about 350.

And that was the Battle of Long Island.

Chapter 5

There were upwards of 8,000 exhausted men crowded into a narrow strip of riverside about a mile and a half long, standing in trenches or crouching behind breast works. The British Army, together with its German hirelings, could easily overrun them in one big rush, any time the order was given. The British Navy could easily pound them to pieces any time the wind changed. They were snared.

Instead of striving to get these beaten men out, Washington reinforced them. He sent over three whole regiments, so that by the morning after the battle there were almost 9,500 crammed into that small space.

Moreover, Washington went over to Brooklyn himself. If the British and the Hessians made that rush or if the navy got up the river now, the commander-in-chief would be in the bag. The war could be ended in half an hour.

There was about an equal number of men, including the sick, still on Manhattan.

In part for its effect upon the enemy, in part for its effect upon his own shaken men, Washington sent all available rifleteers to scattered outposts where they could pop at incautious redcoats.

The redcoats were not used to this. It was a new kind of warfare to them. There were no rifles in the British Army, as there were no sharpshooters. The standard British musket, the Brown Bess, was small, light, and quickly reloaded: a really good infantryman could fire a shot every fifteen seconds. The Brown Bess was not accurate. It was not meant to be. It might carry one hundred yards or even a little farther but its striking power at that range would be trifling, like getting hit with a thrown stone. The musket was used chiefly to terrify the enemy and perhaps bring down a few of them, just before a charge. It was simply pointed in the enemy's general direction; it was not aimed; the Brown Bess did not even have a front sight. Indeed, unless the wind was behind them the redcoats were trained to turn their heads away just before they pulled the trigger. This was to avoid a flashback at the touch hole, which might cost a man his eyes.

The Germans did have riflemen, though not many—a few to each regiment: out of the entire 30,000 mercenaries sent across the Atlantic in the course of the war only about 600 were riflemen. They were called jägers, and they comprised an elite corps, less poorly paid than the rank and file. They were the eyes of the Hessian units, their scouts. For this reason they had to be especially trustworthy men, men who would refrain from bolting, for the average Hessian private would desert at the drop of a tricorne if he was allowed to get far enough away from his commanding officer.

The jägers carried a thick stubby gun, in appearance somewhat like the blunderbuss, but lacking the bell muzzle. It was large-calibered, and threw a ball a considerable distance—say three hundred yards. It had both front and back sights and was much more accurate than the musket. But it took a long time to reload, just because of the rifling; and it could not be fitted with a bayonet.

Though most of those conversant with the Military Art

esteemed the musket as the rifle's superior in battle, nobody doubted that the rifle was by far the better hunting gun. Most of the jägers had been gamekeepers or forest rangers in civilian life, and they were used to this weapon, used to aiming it, used to looking at what they were planning to hit. They were dressed in green, no matter what the color of the regiment to which they were attached. It was well to stay a goodly distance from a man in green.

By the same token, the American riflemen, who came from the frontier, especially the Pennsylvania and Virginia frontiers, generally wore hunting shirts. These were butternut-brown nightshirt-shaped smocks, sometimes fringed at the bottom. There were no rifles on the day of Lexington and Concord. There were none at Breed's Hill.[9] As the siege of Boston wore on, however, small rifle outfits from the frontier began trickling in. These men invariably wore hunting shirts, a costume the British soon learned to respect. This was one reason why Washington urged its general adoption in the Continental Army, as far as could be done. It was cheap; it was convenient; and it inspired respect. In truth, at this time the butternut hunting shirt was the nearest thing to a uniform that the Continental Army *did* have.

The American rifle had been invented and was first made by the descendants of German settlers in western Pennsylvania. (It came to be called the Kentucky rifle, nobody knows why.) It was longer than the jäger's weapon, would carry at least as far, was somewhat more accurate, and took a little more time to reload—because of that long barrel.

The redcoats had started to dig trenches, a pattern of approaches by means of which, within a few days, weather permitting, they would get close to the various small forts without ever having to expose themselves; but the riflemen were like pestiferous mosquitoes. Time after time the redcoats dropped their digging instruments and seized bayonetted

muskets and chased the riflemen from the field; but the riflemen always returned, to pop again.

That was how the first day after the battle, the 28th, was spent. However, that night the northeastern wind that kept the navy away brought rain, great torrents of it. It rained pauselessly and hard for two nights and two days.

It was bitterly cold, and the Americans had no tents or huts. They were unhappy. They were short of rations too, as was so often the case. All they had was hard biscuit and pork, and they had to eat the pork raw, since no fire was possible in that downpour. At the same time, they had to watch the ramparts and man the trenches, which were knee-deep in water. There was no telling when General Howe might change his mind and order a charge.

On the morning of the 27th, at the crest of the battle, at least two regiments of Britishers had had to be restrained by messages from the General himself from following the fugitives into their own lines of fortification and cleaning up the matter then and there. The men fairly *begged* to be allowed to go in, as Howe later reported; but he forbade it. He remembered, it must be assumed, Breed's Hill. He knew how deadly Americans could be when posted behind earthworks. He had time. He would wait for brother Richard, once that wind had shifted.

When the rains came, however, it was, or it should have been, a different story. Despite all sorts of precautions, the cartouche boxes and horns of the shelterless Americans would have been soaked through; and even if there had been a little dry powder left, the flash-pans and the flints and the steel in the strikers all would be wet and would refuse to throw out a spark. There probably were not fifty men in that whole Continental Army who could have fired a single shot if attacked. This applied to the riflemen as well as to those who had muskets, for the locks of both were the same. And very few

Americans had bayonets, whereas all of the British and all of the Hessians save the few jägers had bayonets and had been trained in their vicious use.

Still there was no attack. It would have been a walkover, but it did not come.

The night of August 29–30 was a dark one, fortunately. Washington, who had been in saddle almost continuously for forty-eight hours, was everywhere at once, though he never gave an impression of haste. He had sent to the quartermaster general's office in New York and to General Heath's headquarters at Kingsbridge, ordering all boats available on the East River, whether rowboats or sailboats, to be assembled on the New York shore and sent across to Brooklyn as soon as it became dark. Lest the arrival of these vessels cause a panic among the wet, scared soldiery crowded into that small space between Wallabout and Gowanus bays—soldiers who might smell a retreat—he posted a notice, over his own signature, that the sick would be evacuated along with certain regiments and companies about to be replaced by outfits of similar strength under General Hugh Mercer, who was expected that night. This was false. The Father of his Country *could* tell a lie, when the occasion called for it.

Two Massachusetts regiments, Hutchinson's of Salem and Glover's of Marblehead, were called in from the lines to handle the boats. Virtually all of these men were or had been fishermen or seamen of some sort, and they have been widely praised for the skill with which they worked. Less warm has been the praise of Washington and his aides, who did a magnificent job of staff work that night, and of the soldiers who manned the parapets and trenches, knowing that the rest of the army was slipping away behind them, fearful that there would not be enough time and that they would be sacrificed as a sort of forlorn hope, yet keeping their heads.

Because of the persistence of that unseasonable northeast

The Tide Turns

wind it was feared at first that the sailboats would be of little or no use in ferrying troops to the New York shore, and that at least a handful might indeed be left to their fate. Nevertheless, the work went on hastily, quietly, efficiently. The raw troops were sent first, and it is probable that many of them really did think as they crossed the river that they were being evacuated in order to make room for replacements. Later, it became apparent to even the dullest observer that a full-length retreat was in progress; but by that time most of the edgy ones already had been dispatched.

At about eleven o'clock the northeast wind fell off, and then it swung around to the southwest, where it should have been in the first place. This facilitated the working of the sailing craft. It also meant that soon after the coming of daylight Admiral Howe's advance guard could be expected to come up the East River.

If General Howe was aware of this shift in the wind before he retired for the night—and it is altogether probable that he was notified—he must have gone to sleep with a confident smile on his face, looking forward as he was to seeing brother Richard in the morning.

He had taken his time once too often. He was to be awakened shortly after dawn with the jolting news that a miracle had happened—and there was nothing even in his own book on tactics to tell how to cope with a miracle in the field. The Americans had vanished. Between sundown and sunup, George Washington, as though with the wave of a magic wand, had caused more than 9,000 men to be wafted across the river, complete with equipment—in utter silence. A whole army had been moved, while another army, only a few hundred yards away, knew nothing about it.

To be sure, Washington, with his army united again, had only escaped from a trap of his own making; but he *had* escaped.

In Britain, the news of the Battle of Long Island was received with stupendous acclaim. The court went wild with joy, and King George arranged to confer (with fanfare, if at a distance) the Order of the Bath upon General Howe. All over the land speeches were made, bonfires lit, cannons fired, and there was dancing in the streets. Not only the Tories but also the Whigs were glad that the war was over at last—as obviously it would be, after a bit of minor sweeping up. True, that man Washington still was loose, and his army, his rabble rather, still stuck together; but for all intents and purposes the thing was finished; the jig was up; it just needed one more push.

They did not know George Washington.

CHAPTER

6

THE STICK had been used; now it was time to try the carrot.

That General Howe had been late in starting was not altogether his fault. He had pleaded so piteously for huge reinforcements that he did not dare to leave Staten Island until at least a good part of them had arrived: he was expecting another batch of Hessians right now, near the end of the campaigning season. Nevertheless, and for whatever reason, he *had* been late. Here it was September; and Howe, who did not share the low opinion of Americans held by so many around him, was fearful that the war might drag on for another year. But he and his brother agreed that the time was ripe for a little talk about amnesty and peace.

It was for purely political reasons that the rebels had made a show of defending Brooklyn Heights: this much was obvious. Would they, for the same reasons, put up a show of defending Manhattan? It did not seem likely. They were utterly vulnerable where they sat, as even they must see, for it hardly was possible that they could take their popgun defenses seriously. The General could gobble them up any time he chose. Or would it be better to wait until winter and its weather caused the rebel movement to disintegrate? On the whole, the Howe brothers did not think so. They were in earnest about their role as peace commissioners. They decided to give it another try.

Besides, they had two enemy generals in their grip, an advantage that could hardly have accrued to many commanders in the field—and why not make use of it?

Lord Stirling was not amused. Perhaps to him this business smelled of treason. More likely he just thought to take things easy for a while until he got exchanged. He had many friends in New York, where assuredly his captors would soon be.

Sullivan, however, listened with rapt attention, his lawyer's instinct roused.

(It never failed to tickle the British officers that American high-rankers were that only in wartime, and were all sorts of other grotesque, not to say vulgar, things in times of peace: Mühlenberg the minister, Glover the fish dealer, Greene the blacksmith, and the stationer Knox, the hatter Barton. To them an officer was an officer, and that's *what* he was, that and no more. But General Mercer was a physician, General Putnam a farmer, General Wheedon a tavern keeper, and General Sullivan, it proved, was an attorney.)

So Sullivan was induced to give his parole and go to Philadelphia, to explain to the Continental Congress the peacemaking powers entrusted by His Majesty to the Howe brothers. He was not well received. John Adams snorted that the man was no more than "a decoy duck whom Lord Howe had sent among us to seduce us into a renunciation of our independence."

Adams, feeling that way, might have been expected to refuse to be on a three-man committee the Congress—after considerable debate—appointed to listen to the Howes; and indeed he did try to get out of it, but he was persuaded to serve. The other members were Edward Rutledge, of South Carolina, and Benjamin Franklin. They left Philadelphia September 10, Adams on horseback, the other two in "chairs,"[10] and arrived at Perth Amboy, just across from Staten Island, the next morning. Though headquarters was in despair because of the rate of desertion from the Continental Army—whole companies were walking away, whole regiments at a time—these travelers across the waist of New Jersey noted with approval that the roads were clogged with militiamen on their way to New York.

At the mouth of the Raritan there were waiting a boat, oarsmen, and a British officer. The latter clearly was intended to serve as a hostage for the return of the three Congressmen —not much of a swap; but they scoffed at this and asked him to come along on the trip to Staten Island. He was amazed to meet with such politeness.

Admiral Lord Howe greeted them right on the beach—a singular mark of courtesy—and escorted them to the nearby Billop House, his headquarters. He apologized for the absence of his brother the general, whose duties kept him on Long Island.

A Hessian regiment was on guard duty at the Billop House, and, Adams reports, "We walked up to the house between lines of grenadiers, looking fierce as ten furies, and making all the grimaces, and gestures, and motions of their muskets which, (I suppose,) military etiquette requires, but which we neither understood nor regarded."[11]

Lord Howe tactfully refrained from talking business until after lunch, which consisted of mutton, tongue, cold ham, bread, and a really good claret. There were present, besides the Admiral and the congressmen, the colonel of the regiment on guard duty and Lord Howe's personal secretary, neither of whom had much to say. Immediately afterward, the colonel bowed himself out, pleading professional obligations, and the secretary fetched forth his writing materials.

Howe did most of the talking. He started by saying how grateful he was to the Americans who had caused to be erected a memorial to his late beloved brother, and how grieved he would be if the colonial cause went to pieces. Franklin, deadpan, murmured: "We will use our utmost endeavors to save your lordship that mortification."

If none of the committeemen seemed to take this talk seriously it was because Lord Howe—who after all had suggested it—was, again, vague to the point of being almost unintelligible. He *sounded* conciliatory, but he offered nothing; and when the congressmen pointed out that Great Britain might well have more to gain by easy and profitable relations with independent ex-colonies than she would have by keeping those colonies in chains, he shook his head impatiently, changing the subject. He had no authority to discuss independence. The very word made him wince.

The truth is, my lord was not sure of himself. The orders he had received from his cousin the King were not the orders he would have wanted. They were much too restrictive, and if it had been possible to carry them through they would have put the colonies into a position of utter, outright subservience to Great Britain. Admiral Howe knew this, and he knew too that he could not read those orders aloud to these men. He was concealing something all the time, and this—for he was in essence honest—made him uneasy.

For instance, he made no mention of the written demand that the colonies give "guarantees" of their future good behavior, "guarantees" that this sort of thing would not happen again. Just what these "guarantees" were to be, and who would fix them, and when, his orders did not say. There was one exception. The orders specifically stated that before there could be any reconciliation the two colonies that operated under the most liberal charters—Connecticut and Rhode Island—must give up those charters. This only goes to show how stupid, how unrealistic, was the King—or his advisors. Those charters had been in operation for almost two hundred years, and there wasn't a man in either state, not even the most rabid Tory, who would not have given his life to keep them. George III, it would seem, had started out with the assumption that the erring colonies would see the faults of their ways and would return on their knees.

"Pardon" was a word often on his lordship's lips, but he did not explain that his secret orders carried a list of exceptions, the names of men who on no account whatsoever would be pardoned, and that one of these was John Adams. Did his lordship see, in his mind's eye, a rope around the neck of one of his luncheon guests? If so, he did not mention it.

No time was wasted. Lord Howe soon ran out of words —he was anything but a glib man—and the visitors made it abundantly clear that they could not even start to discuss details unless and until the independence of the thirteen colonies was conceded. Lord Howe, sighing, shook his head; and they all rose, and bowed to one another; and a few minutes later, complete with oarsmen and an officer carrying a flag of truce, the congressmen were on their way back to Perth Amboy.

The carrot was laid aside; the stick was taken up again.

Brother William had been speaking no less than the truth when he pleaded that army matters kept him away from the Billop House. He was a busy man, though it did not seem so to the soldiers and civilians still in New York, who every day expected an attack. Though he had command of all the waters surrounding New York, though he had fanned out all over the western end of Long Island, and though the Continental Army would seem to be falling apart before his very eyes and in any event was spread painfully thin, General Howe allowed more than two weeks to pass before he struck.

He had not been twiddling his thumbs in that time. Even if brother Richard struck some sort of agreement with those rebel leaders over on Staten Island, it behoved him, brother William, to be ready to snatch the city. He could of course have hammered it to pieces from Brooklyn Heights with the forty big guns he had brought along, but what good would that do him? He would only be reducing to rubble a town that might otherwise make a snug winter quarters for him and his men. Sooner or later, anyway, the place would have to be taken by hand, as it were. And Howe had the men.

He sought to strike, when he did strike, with overwhelming force. This meant boats, many boats, more than could be supplied by the various frigates and bomb ketches that were already in the East River. He had to bring these small boats from the fleet, which lay in lower New York Bay. Here, exactly, was his trouble. The East River for most of its length is only about half a mile wide. To tack up it with a sailing boat of any kind meant venturing perilously close to the New York shore, where the rebels had batteries. On the other hand, to row a large number of boats along the Long Island shore would be to invite cannonballs from those same batteries. The work, then, would have to be done at night. And conditions were only favorable during certain hours.

For the East River, though it has always been called that, is not a river at all but a tidal estuary extending from upper New York Bay to Long Island Sound. Sometimes it flows north, sometimes south; and always it flows fast. When it flowed south Howe could not possibly move his small boats north, even at night—no matter what the wind. So it took time.

Washington could not count upon that time, but he made as much of it as possible. He was reorganizing his army,

The Tide Turns

as much of it as had held together. Recruits were pouring in all the time, true, but they were virtually without equipment, often without arms, and the increase was more than offset by desertions. The Connecticut militia, for example, which had numbered about 6,000 at the time of the battle of Long Island, had melted to 2,000 within a couple of weeks.

Washington issued an order that the roll should be called three times a day; but this did little good when the man who was supposed to call it had himself deserted.

Desperate, the commander-in-chief wrote to Congress, pleading that a central Continental army be organized to replace the various bits-and-pieces militia, and urging that it be enlisted for the duration, not for just a few months at a time. Congress agreed, and authorized eighty-five regiments with five-year enlistment terms; but such an army, if it was even possible, could never be raised and trained in time to save New York.

Washington was sure that New York was doomed, but he understood that the Congress wanted him to defend every foot of it for as long as possible.

Greene was back on duty after his sick leave, and Greene, whom the commander-in-chief greatly trusted, unequivocally advocated the evacuation of New York. He would do more than that. He'd burn the whole city before leaving it, so that the British could not use it for winter quarters. Others favored the same action, among them some of New York's largest landowners. (Only a few months earlier, before Boston, John Hancock, easily the biggest property owner of that city, was urging Washington to burn *it*.)

Congress specifically forbade the burning of New York. The city might be lost; but Congress was confident that it would be recovered.

Howe was getting ready, gradually. He was bringing up those boats. He was patrolling the East River. He had taken over Montressor's Island and Buchanan's Island.[12] He was assembling and hiring pilots.

Washington called a council of war, which determined to hold on to New York at all costs, but soon afterward he called another council, which reversed this decision, advising the commander-in-chief to evacuate all his stores, if not his troops.

He started to do this; but he was too late.

September 15 (it was a Sunday) Howe struck.

CHAPTER

7

THE MORNING was hot and clear. It threatened mugginess. Soon after dawn five warships took up north-and-south posts parallel to the East River shore of Manhattan at a point called Kip's Bay, some miles above the town itself.[13] Because this had been identified as a possible landing place, a few hundred Connecticut militiamen were stationed there in shallow open trenches, mere scooped-out slits with the dirt piled on the riverside. They had no fieldpieces. They had no tents. They were under the command of a Captain William Douglas, and none of them had ever been under fire. What is more, because of some characteristic flubbery of the supply department they had not been issued rations for twenty-four hours; and in that time they had eaten only such few acorns as they could find in the woods behind them—when they were supposed to be manning the trenches.

Against such wretches the British Navy opened its might. It was like using a sledge hammer to swat a fly.

The flatboats came first, emerging from hiding places along the Long Island shore and especially from the mouth of Newtown Creek. There were eighty-four of these flatboats, probably the same ones that had been used to make the landing on Long Island three weeks before, and each was crammed to the gunnels with soldiers. They did not cross the whole river, but huddled for temporary protection behind the warships.

This was a little after ten o'clock. At a little before eleven the warships opened up with all their broadsides at once. There were seventy-some guns, big ones, and the noise and the smoke were terrific: old navy men themselves said that they had never before known anything like it.

The guns did not speak long. They did not need to. As soon as they fell silent the flatboats started forth again, long oars glittering in the sun. The first ones held the cream of the redcoats, the light-infantry units, specially trained for just such attacks. To one frightened spectator they looked like "a clover field in full bloom."

The boats bumped the shore. The redcoats tumbled out and scrambled up the rocks, ready for anything.

What they found was a litter of thrown-away muskets, knapsacks, blankets—nothing else, no men. The Connecticut militia had decamped without firing a shot.

Their action was noticed by several similar companies of raw troops stationed south of them, who followed their example, though nobody was attacking *them*. The panic—and it could only be called that—was on.

Everybody wanted to get back of the fortifications at Harlem.

There were two roads north from New York. They were one until they split, a few miles out of town. The left one, called the Bloomingdale road, more or less paralleled the Hudson River all the way to Harlem. The other, the (Boston) Post road, more or less paralleled the East River, and it led to King's Bridge, the extreme northern tip of the island.[14]

The men who broke cover along the East River all made for the Post road, which was the nearer to them.

The Tide Turns

Washington, still believing that the real attack would come eventually from King's Bridge—it was the logical way to do the job, wrapping up the whole Continental Army from the north—was in Harlem, "a sweet little village with one church," when the bombardment first was heard. He leapt on his horse and started south down the Post road. It seemed incredible that the British should interpose a force, no matter how big it was, between two Continental forces, a direct violation of the rules of the Military Act. Yet from the sound of those guns that is exactly what they were trying to do: they were trying to cut the island in half. Anyway, that's where the shooting was, so that was where Washington belonged. He rode hard, surrounded by his staff.

When he reached the place where the lane traversed the island at its waist, so to speak, connecting the Post road with the Bloomingdale road, he came upon the first of the panickers.

It was a sight to take the heart out of any general. The men, officers and all, had given in to fright. They were not even making any show of defense. They simply ran, most of them without weapons. They were shameless. They were pop-eyed.

Washington went wild. He drew his sword and slapped right and left with its flat. He cursed. He screamed with rage—this man who usually had such perfect control of himself. He slammed his hat to the ground. Nobody ever had seen him act this way. His very aides were frightened.

"Take the fence! Take the cornfield!" he cried.[15]

A few obeyed, and for a moment it looked as if it might be possible to stage some sort of stand—especially as there was no enemy in sight—but just then a force of a few hundred Hessians came marching up from the south.

These Hessians were not planning to close any trap. They were simply carrying out their orders, marching slowly north along the general line of the East River, taking a few prisoners here and there, the outflung jägers occasionally popping at fugitives just for the fun of it.

The mere sight of them was enough. Horrendous rumors still swirled—and were believed—about the butchery these German beasts had committed among prisoners at Brooklyn Heights (where, as a matter of fact, they had behaved themselves very well), and nobody paused to put these to the proof. The few rallying Continentals gave up as one man. They spun about, dropping everything, and soon were again racing up the Post road or streaming across the fields to the north.

It was an utter rout.

Washington was left alone with his staff.

"Are these the men I am to protect America with?" he cried.

His rage faded as suddenly as it had come. He seemed like one who had been dazed by a blow on the head. He turned his horse slowly to face the oncoming Hessians—who had not unshouldered their muskets or quickened their pace or made any other truculent gesture—and for a moment he sat looking at them. He might have been thinking of riding into them and ending his life, in that moment.

An aide quietly took a rein and turned the steed about; and with no other word, the commander-in-chief allowed himself to be led back up the Post road toward the fortifications of Harlem Heights.

One of those who had been a member of the commander-in-chief's party—Washington had been holding a council of war in the Morris House—was General Israel Putnam, the Indian fighter. In the recent reorganization of the Continental Army he had been given command of the southernmost division, stationed in and around the town of New York itself. His men might well be cornered. There were 3,000 of them, almost a third of the effectives in the whole army, and they had sixty-seven cannons, or more than half of those on the Continental side.

Old Put was fat, and he was fifty-eight, going on fifty-nine—but he knew his duty when he saw it. His place was with his men. He galloped south.

The work of evacuating supplies from the town had already begun, but it had gone slowly because of the lack of horses. There were still many such supplies left in New York, and there was nothing that Old Put could do about them now. Nor would he be able to get the guns out, and it was not likely that he would even have time to spike them properly. But he must do whatever he could for the men.

All was confusion among the Americans, who were intent upon one thing only—to get to cover in Harlem; but the British seemed to know what they were doing. The flatboats had been sent back promptly, to fetch a second wave of troopers. Those already landed, about 5,000 at a quick estimate, found themselves, to their own amazement, with no fighting to do. Some were told off to go down the shore of the East River, others were sent up north, their orders being to drive out or perhaps only to report such pockets of resistance as might present themselves. They were finding none of these. They moved slowly.

Another body of men—among them it would seem the headquarters unit—had moved straight inland, climbing a hill that, with the house on its summit, was called Inclenberg. This house was owned by a wealthy Quaker named Robert Murray, who, like most wealthy men, was a Tory, and who, for this reason, had taken himself elsewhere.[16] Here they had halted.

This much Old Put was able to take in, as he gave the Inclenberg a wide berth. If they pushed west from that point, he could see, he and his men were lost. If they stayed there a

ISRAEL ("OLD PUT") PUTNAM

while he had some chance of getting out—if he could get a good guide.

In the town, too, all was confusion. There were few civilians left, and what there were kept under cover, praying for the best, but the officers were at loggerheads as to what course to take in the absence of their general. They were mostly artillerymen, and the arguments were about whether or not the guns should be spiked and abandoned or whether they should be kept intact in the fortlets built according to plans laid down by Major General Lee—who, with his dogs, was still proceeding north in a blaze of glory—and fought for to the last man. Some said that this would be sheer suicide and would in any event do nothing even to inconvenience the redcoats. Others demurred.

Old Put settled the matter by ordering an immediate abandonment of everything and the start of a march north on the west side of the island.

The west side, in town and above it, was by no means as well built up, as heavily populated, as the east side, where the greatest part of the business was. Putnam himself knew almost nothing about it. He only knew the Post road, which now was occupied by the enemy, on the east side.

He was lucky. It turned out that one of his own aides, a young fellow named Burr, Aaron Burr, had been born in this town and knew every foot of it and of the land to the north, east side as well as west side. Also, young Burr was not a man to lose his head. You could depend upon him.

It is not known, but it has been surmised, that Captain Burr, somewhere in the midst of this dust-choked turmoil, found himself giving orders to another young captain, this one a cannoneer, Alexander Hamilton. They were strangely alike, these two. Each was only twenty, and short, slight of build, delicate, high-strung, with sandy hair, with a determined chin, and damn-you eyes. One had gone to the College of New Jersey, the other to King's College,[17] but both were law students. Each, a dainty dresser, cocked his tricorne low over his eyes in front, as was the macaroni mode. They might have been twins.

There is no proof that they did meet face to face, but it *could* have happened. If so, it was for the first time. It would not be for the last.

The day was furiously hot, and it was close. The dust was blinding. The column, when at last they got it formed, was two miles long. The men stayed in it, too. For all their thirst they refrained from falling out to sample wells or to raid orchards. They seemed to sense the seriousness of their situation. The Bloomingdale road was narrow. They would have had no room, if attacked in flank, to draw up proper battle lines. But despite all the dust they kicked up, they were not detected.

Howe decided to take the main part of his army north to camp on the plain just below Harlem. He used the Post road for this, and his column too was about two miles long—for the Post road was much wider than the Bloomingdale road. At one time, and for several hours, these two columns were marching in the same direction with less than two miles between them; yet, despite the dust, neither knew that the other was over there.[18]

Putnam's men, led by Burr, and with Old Put himself galloping back and forth, started from a point farther south than the British column, and they went to a point farther north. They had marched twelve miles in all, in the middle of one of the hottest days on record.

The British at least got to their camping site in time to run up tents before the cloudburst that had for some time been threatening. The Americans were still on the road, where all the dust was turned into mucilaginous mud. Nor did they have tents when they *did* get to camp. They didn't have anything.

All the same, they had been lucky. They might have been dead or incarcerated in prison hulks by that time, if only Howe had not decided to wait a while at the Inclenberg.

Why did he?

The question has fascinated historians. It will never be accurately answered. The fond believers in fables should be reminded, however, that Howe had got to the Murray House much sooner than he expected. He had supposed that the rebels would put up *some* kind of fight. He simply could not understand men who would break and run without firing a shot. The lack of delay had thrown his schedule out of kilter. In any case, he had given orders that a pause should be made at the Inclenberg, the only high place for miles around, an excellent site from which to survey the field, and a place to wait until the second division had been landed. After all, he did not know that Putnam and 3,000 Continentals were in a trap. How could he know that? So he stuck to his original plan.

This explanation is too simple for the myth-makers, who prefer to picture Mrs. Murray as a sort of colonial Cleopatra who fed General Howe wine and cakes, flirted with him, and laughed enticingly at his sallies, in a desperate attempt to save Israel Putnam and his men. It is astonishing how many have swallowed this story.[19] It just doesn't jell.

In the first place, Mrs. Murray could hardly have known that Old Put had plunged into the lower-Manhattan bag all of his own accord. He didn't know it himself until the last minute. Again, she was a Quaker, and as such disapproved of war, and a Tory, who as *such* disapproved of rebellion. Moreover, she was in her fifties and the mother of twelve children, hardly one to turn seductress at a moment's notice.

Anyway, the men were safe—for the present.

Chapter 8

It would soon be winter; already the nights were nippy. In the chill predawn of the 16th, the day after the disgrace at Kip's Bay, Washington, still awake, busy again, surveyed his position and determined to send out a scouting force.

The position, previously selected, was a strong one; but he had lost faith in the 25,000 men—actually only a little over 16,000 effectives—who served under him. Would they stand, if attacked? Or would they bolt, as they had done the day before? Even Howe, who was known to disapprove of frontal attacks against strong positions except as a measure of desperation, might decide upon such an attack this morning, meaning to take advantage of the weariness, the wetness, the discouragement of the Continentals.

From where he was, Washington could not see into the British camp, but he knew that it was not far away. His own battered army occupied the northern third of Manhattan Island, which was generally narrow here. His north was the Harlem River and the bridge at King's Bridge, which he held with a large force lest he be flanked from that direction. In his center, near the Hudson's shore, was massive Fort Washington, garrisoned by fully 2,000 men, despite the fact that it had already proved its inability, together with Fort Constitution across the river (the name of this, it had just been agreed, should be changed to Fort Lee, in honor of the returned hero), to stop the passage of warships. His east was Long Island Sound and the tricky Hell Gate, his west the Hudson. It was south that he faced this morning, for the south held the British.

The British and their German auxiliaries were all unruffled by the romp of yesterday. They had enjoyed a good dry sleep; and undoubtedly they were now about to enjoy a good hot breakfast. They controlled both rivers, and their supply line was invulnerable. Would they try to crash the three parallel lines of fortification that Washington had previously set up to guard Harlem Heights,[20] itself a naturally strong position? He had to find out.

For this purpose he selected Colonel Thomas Knowlton, a Connecticut man who had recently organized an unconventional but decidedly dashing company of young men called the Rangers. The Rangers were meant for scouting, for spying if necessary, for any kind of dangerous assignment that called for a cool head and controlled courage. They were mostly from Connecticut, all handpicked, all volunteers. Knowlton himself was thirty-six, a tall, darkhaired, handsome, quiet man. He had served under Putnam in the French and Indian War, and had been one of the heroes of Bunker Hill and of Long Island. He never raised his voice. His men adored him. (One of those men, young Captain Nathan Hale, only the other day had volunteered for a perilous mission of spying behind the British lines in Long Island, where, as far as anybody in the American camp knew, he still was.)

The Rangers had not been involved in the late stampede. They had been stationed on the east coast of Harlem, where Washington, at that time, expected the assault.

Knowlton set forth with about 120 men, and at first light they climbed down Harlem Heights, past the various lines of fortification, past the farthest-out pickets, to the plain below. Here, near a stone farmhouse, they encountered a group of about 400 British light infantry.

These light infantry, in the British Army, were one of the classifications of soldiers—the grenadiers without grenades were the other—known as flank companies, because on paper they guarded the flanks of a given regiment. Actually, they usually worked by themselves or with the light infantry or grenadiers from other regiments. They were picked men, who expected to be sent on tough missions. (Most of those dispatched from Boston to destroy the supplies at Concord, for instance, had been light infantry, though there had been a few grenadier units.) They were, in effect, the enemy's Rangers, the nearest thing that the rigid British Army permitted in the way of irregulars. They were men to be watched.

In this case, they attacked immediately.

Knowlton's men took up positions behind a stone wall and defended themselves with verve, even with nonchalance, for more than an hour, though outnumbered by more than three to one. Then, having lost a few men, but having learned what they had come out to learn, they made an orderly retreat to the American outposts.

There they were greeted by a considerable clump of officers, including several generals, who had been attracted by the sound of musketry. They were praised. The British, however, had only jeers for their late opponents. The British stopped at a sensible distance, and before they prepared to turn back they had their bugler blow the call that signified that the fox has gone to earth. It was deliberate, and an error. It was too much. There were fox hunters among the Continentals—George Washington himself, for one—who resented this impertinence. The commander-in-chief, right there on the field, in saddle, decided to teach the enemy better manners.

He laid his plans quickly, a most unorthodox proceeding then. He sent forth a force about equal to that of the taunting light infantry. *They* would not know the difference, since none of the Continentals wore uniforms anyway; they would simply assume that the men they had chased off the field were coming back, reinforced, for more. They would ask nothing better than a good stand-up fight.

Meanwhile, Knowlton's Rangers, together with another body of about the same strength, Major Andrew Leitch's riflemen, lately arrived from Virginia, were to slip around to the left—the British right—where the ground was rough and cover was plentiful. They were to close in on the British from the rear, taking them by surprise. It would have been a prize package.

The trick came within an ace of working. What spoiled it was that some of the green riflemen got excited and started to shoot before they were supposed to. The British, who could think on their feet, whirled about, saw what was up, and ran. They did not retreat in step, facing backward toward the enemy, their muskets at port position; they sprinted.

A great cheer went up from the Continentals. So the redcoats had backs after all!

The redcoats did not go far. When they saw that they were safely out of the trap—the Rangers and the riflemen had joined the others in pushing forward—they took up a position in a field of buckwheat, sent for reinforcements, and continued to fight.

The reinforcements came on the run, literally. They were the famous 42nd Highlanders, the Black Watch. Right after them, also trotting, came a large detachment of jägers. Washington too reinforced his men. Whether on the inspira-

THE BATTLE OF HARLEM

tion of the moment or simply because they happened to be near at hand, one of the regiments he sent in was that of the Connecticut militiamen under Douglas, the quitters of Kip's Bay. Today, with full bellies, they behaved beautifully.

The struggle went on, at forty to fifty yards' range, with neither side willing to back away. Leitch and Knowlton both fell, within a few minutes of each other, but their men went right on firing, the company officers taking over.[21]

The fracas might have developed into a full-length battle, something neither general wanted, had not Washington, at about two o'clock in the afternoon, sent out an order to withdraw. The men raged, but they obeyed.

The British, in no hurry to pursue, stood their ground until it became evident that the rebels did not mean to return, and then they marched back to their own camp.

The Tide Turns

The action had been inconclusive. No goal had been attained, no position held or taken, and the losses, which were slight, were about evenly balanced. British historians call it merely a skirmish, and laugh at Americans who refer to it as the *Battle* of Harlem Heights. Nevertheless, it meant a great deal in the Continental camp. Americans had stood toe-to-toe with Hessians and redcoats and also kilted Scots, and slugged it out by the hour. Twice the enemy had retreated a short distance—once, to be sure, because they saw that they were almost in a trap, the second time because they were running out of ammunition—but they *had* retreated.

Still, the satisfaction that this gave did not slow the coming of winter. There was enough firewood in the Continental camp, what with the woods that stippled the landscape and what with the farmers' rail fences, but there were not enough tents, blankets, pots, kettles. Nor was there enough food. Sickness was worse than ever. There was an epidemic of thievery, and courts-martial sat all day. Though new militiamen stumbled in, many of them without weapons, much less cooking equipment, those present went on deserting. Men were saying that maybe they had better not wait until their short terms of enlistment had expired, that George Washington just didn't seem to know his business, and that maybe *now* was the time to go, while they could still get home, and before they had been completely surrounded by redcoats.

Three days after the fight at Harlem Heights the Howe brothers issued a declaration urging Americans "to return to their allegiance, accept the blessing of peace, and to be secured in a free enjoyment of their liberty and properties." The brothers clearly hoped that they were going over the heads of the Congress, which they did not trust, to the American people themselves, the real people. But they were characteristically and perhaps necessarily vague, and their declaration did not have much effect, if it had any effect at all.

The day after that, New York burned down—or, at least, about a tenth of it did, a central tenth, completely, 493 houses and other buildings. Most of these had cedar shingles, and there was a strong south wind. Of course the British blamed the rebels for this, while the rebels blamed the British. In fact, almost certainly it was an accident. It greatly inconvenienced the occupying troops, but it did nothing to improve the spirits of those encamped on Harlem Heights.

Two days later, Captain Hale was hanged as a spy before the gates of the big artillery park near the Post road north of town.[22] Word of the event reached the Continental camp, where he had many friends. It was reported that he'd been caught red-handed in New York, notes and plans hidden on his person, and also that he had gone well, having only expressed regret that he had but one life to give for his country. The American cause certainly needed a martyr, but just at that time it did not seem to matter to the men on Harlem Heights. They were too tired to care. They wanted to go home.

And what was General Howe doing, along military lines, in the four weeks that followed the fighting at Harlem? He was doing the worst thing possible for the Continental Army. He was doing—nothing.

Chapter

9

"It is better to dig a ditch every morning and fill it up at night than to have the men idle," Israel Putnam had said at the siege of Boston. But now the men were tired of their shovels and picks. Months of back-breaking labor had gone into those breastworks in lower Manhattan, all of which had been abandoned within an hour. The men could have used some drill, certainly; but who was there to drill them? Their own officers knew only the most rudimentary movements of what was then called "the discipline" and later was to be known as the manual of arms; and even their officers did not dare to demand.

The process was known as "levelling" and it was very democratic, perhaps too democratic to be workable. It was most prevalent among the New England outfits, and it shocked Southerners. The militiamen, in short, elected their own officers, and if they did not like the way those appointees behaved they demoted them. In consequence, a militia officer deferred to his men. He all but groveled before them. He was always afraid to give an unpleasant order. The best he could hope for was to hold them together, to keep them from walking out of camp in disgust, as so many were doing in Harlem Heights right then.

If there had been any action they might not have waxed restless, but Howe had not yet made up his mind about what he would do next, so the men lolled around, finding fault.

Meanwhile the generals conferred. The Continental forces were spread too thin, as Washington knew—they all knew that. Yet Howe any day might move with overwhelming strength from the Hudson on the west, from New York to the south, or from the East River. All of these points, and the north as well, had to be covered. In addition, it was thought necessary to man each of the big forts with about 2,000 men. *Why*, since their uselessness had been demonstrated, it is hard to see—unless it was because the faraway Congress urged it. Lee, who had recently rejoined the army, argued against staying in the admittedly precarious position in which they now found themselves. He would have moved out of Manhattan, Fort Washington and all, and assembled the now scattered forces at some strong place in Westchester County, there to wait, as they had to wait, for Howe's next stroke. Nathanael Greene thought that the forts ought to be held, and even reinforced. Greene was usually right in military matters; but he was dead wrong this time.

October 12, Howe moved. He led a large force up the East River and through Hell Gate in a fog—a delicate bit of shiphandling—and landed at Throg's Neck.

Excepting on Long Island, where there were so many Tories, Howe's intelligence service was scarcely superior to that of Washington, which, after the Nathan Hale failure, was just about nonexistent. Seemingly, Howe had been led to believe that Throg's Neck, directly east of the Continental lines, *was* a neck—that is, a small peninsula. This it was not, except at low tide. The rest of the time it was an island.

The mainland was reached from Throg's Neck by means

of a ford and a small wooden bridge. The British tried the bridge first. Two dozen Pennsylvania riflemen rose from behind a woodpile at its mainland end and started to shoot. The British—their muskets would not carry that far—turned and ran for cover.

Then the British tried the ford, and their reception was much the same.

Both places of defense were promptly reinforced, and in a very short time the Americans had 1,800 men ready to dispute the passage.

The actual landing went on all this while, for the British apparently were committed to the place, island or no island. They started to dig in.

Howe himself arrived, looked things over, and decided that a push here would cost too much. But he had no thought of turning back. He just pitched camp and waited six days for his baggage to catch up to him.

All of this caused consternation among the American generals, who held another council in Washington's Harlem headquarters on October 16. Though Howe had left a strong occupying force in New York, under Lord Percy, there was little chance of an attack from the south; neither had the British been busy in the Hudson; but with the greatest part of the British and Hessian troops at Throg's Neck, where they were clearly preparing to outflank the Continentals from the north and drive them against the Hudson, there were only two things for the Continentals to do—fight against odds and in an unfavorable position, or get out. The generals decided to get out. They would retreat to White Plains, in Westchester County, a territory that had already been reconnoitred with exactly this in mind. The question was not to-retreat-or-not-retreat. The question was whether to abandon Fort Washington at the same time, or to leave it to be completely surrounded by the enemy, though the place did not even have its own well—and White Plains was fifteen miles away. What Washington thought about it we do not know, and probably never will learn,[23] but after some discussion the council decided to try to hold onto the fort. That was a tragic mistake.

The retreat was started immediately, and it was a laborious one. Because of a shortage of both horses and wagons the supplies had to be moved in relays, while the guns were hauled by hand. Adequately equipped, the army could have made that jump in one good day. As it was, it took four.

There was always a chance that it would not get there at all. There was a chance that Howe might move rapidly, for a change, and hook around to the north of an army woefully spread out, an army it could then squash piecemeal.

Howe did bestir himself on October 18, when he sailed three miles east to Pell's Point,[24] a place that he had no doubt was on the mainland. There he landed 4,000 men unopposed. But he was watched. Colonel John Glover, a short, laconic man from Marblehead, "a tough little terrier of a man,"[25] had four small regiments with him, all, like Glover himself, Massachusetts Yankees, about 750 of them. He was posted at Eastchester, a mile away.

Glover, though he looked calm, as was his duty, was not sure of himself. After all, he had seen little action. What he knew as a commanding officer was only what he had learned on the village green drilling the militia—his friends, his neighbors. He wished fervently (as he was to confess later) that he had been accompanied by an expert, like, say, Charles Lee.

He did all right by himself. He was only expected to delay the enemy, not stop them, as he perfectly understood. He posted his men by regiments behind a series of stone walls. The enemy, mostly Hessians in the advance guard, had reached a point within fifty yards of the first wall before the Americans showed themselves by rising suddenly and starting

The Tide Turns

to shoot. By the time the Hessians had recovered, and loaded their muskets, and fixed their bayonets, and were preparing to charge, the Americans quietly faded away. At the next wall the same thing happened, and at the next, and so on all day. At one time the enemy suspended action for more than two hours until the main body of British troops could be brought up and deployed.

Howe, though he had got off to an early start, made only three miles that day. And Glover's men, nothing in their stomachs but no doubt with grins across their faces, slept on the bare ground.

There was to be another deed of derring-do before White Plains was reached. Major Robert Rogers was camped with his much-hated Rangers—the Americans looked upon them as renegades—about five miles from the British right, near the village of Mamaroneck, the night of Tuesday, October 22. There were about 500 of them, and it was decided to try to cut them out. Colonel John Haslet and his daredevil Delawareans, who had fought so gallantly on Long Island, were reinforced by sundry Maryland and Virginia units, so that there were about 750 of them in all. Because in the darkness they stumbled upon a large outpost—it had been a last-minute thought on the part of Rogers—the cutting-out party was, theoretically, a failure. But it did boost spirits. There was some hard and nasty night fighting, and the Americans, with trifling losses of their own, did kill a few Rangers and did take thirty-six prisoners, and they also captured a pair of colors, about sixty muskets, and (most welcome of all) a large supply of blankets.

Howe was one of the outstanding feet-draggers of military history. He spent four days and four nights at Mamaroneck, and before that he had spent three days at New Rochelle. When at last he did arrive before Washington's position at White Plains, on the 28th, he had taken ten days to go seventeen miles. He *said* that he was waiting for reinforcements, though he already outnumbered his enemy, and it is true that on the day that he landed at Pell's Point 120 vessels cast anchor in lower New York Bay, bringing him 3,400 British, 3,997 Hessians, 670 Waldeckers, and an odd company of jägers. However, the British, raw recruits, were kept in New York for garrison duty, while the Waldeckers, Hessians, and jägers were sent only to New Rochelle, which they were instructed to hold—but who could have threatened it?—in the absence of the General. They took no part in the battle that was about to ensue.

This battle was preceded by yet another from-behind-stone-walls peppering, this time on the part of six New England regiments who played hob with several Hessian outfits until the Hessians rallied and prepared to charge, whereupon the New Englanders quietly retired to the protection of their own lines.

It is notable that Howe was "shoving" the Hessians. This was in part, surely, because they were costing his country a pretty penny and he wanted to get his money's worth, but it was also due to the insistence of the Hessian officers, who were thirsty for strife, for a chance to garner some "glory"— an appreciable asset in their profession. What the rank and file thought, if they thought at all, did not, of course, matter.

The engagement itself was a lively one, though nothing new, and conducted on a comparatively small scale. The British wrapped up the American right wing, on the far side of the Bronx River, by means of a frontal attack heavily supported by artillery, of which they had a preponderance, and, for the first time against Americans, by cavalry.[26]

The British and Hessians behaved well throughout, as was to be expected. The Americans behaved badly sometimes, at other times extremely well. A Connecticut militia regiment broke and ran when one of its members was killed by a high-flying cannonball—though the redcoats were not near—and it was only with difficulty persuaded to return to the field. On the other hand, Haslet's memorable Delawareans, Ritzema's New Yorkers, and Smallwood's Marylanders covered themselves with glory, the Delawareans in particular backing away "sullenly" when all support had fallen from them.

Who won the battle? History calls it a British victory, and this decision will do as well as any. The British and Hessians, undeniably, killed and wounded and took prisoner more Americans than the Americans did of them—many more. Which is one way to figure it. The Hessians and the British seized and held the field, which is another. But the field itself meant nothing to them. Their grand object, their only object really, was to get in back of the Continental Army and smash it; and this they did not succeed in doing.

Washington, when he saw that his right was threatened, retreated to a prepared line behind the village of White Plains, and a little later—and this was no mean feat when his front was under fire—he safely retreated to, and took over, a third prepared position several miles away.

Howe did not attack him in this third position, ever. Howe had had enough for one day. He started back to New York.

Washington still had an army: that was the only thing that counted. It might not have been much of an army, but such as it was it existed.

CHAPTER

10

There was a Mrs. Howe at home, but the General did not mope on that account. Not garrulous, neither was he glum; but he was a man who liked good clothes, good food, good wine and plenty of it, and other creature comforts. In Boston he had met a Mrs. Joshua Loring, nee Lloyd, who was described as tall, almost as tall as the General himself, and "a dazzling blonde." The lady was willing, and her husband, a loyalist, had no objection, especially after Howe had seen to it that he was given a sinecure; and so an affair was launched.

After the evacuation of Boston, the Sultana—as the boys around headquarters came to call her—accompanied her lover to Halifax. When he invaded New York she followed soon after. He made no bones about the thing. He rode out with her in a carriage. He went to the theatre with her, and to the officers' balls. He sat up all night at the gambling table with her: they were both passionately fond of gambling.[27]

What the folks in Halifax thought of this is not a matter of record, but Bostonians surely disapproved, and even the remaining residents of New York, at that time esteemed the most blasé of all American cities, clucked their tongues and shook their heads. You just didn't do things like that in a decent place.

The General paid them no mind; and after the scuffling at White Plains he was understandably eager to get back to his mistress in town. However, there was a job to be done on the way. There was Fort Washington.

It was not a fort at all, really: it was just a fortified hill. The *position* was a strong one. The peak of Mount Washington[28] was almost two hundred feet above the Hudson River, into which at this point a fortified promontory, Jeffery's Hook, jutted. That river was on the west; on the north and east there was the less formidable Harlem River. The south, Harlem Heights, was protected by Washington's triple lines. On all four sides the slopes were sharp, rocky, and thickly wooded. This was a great deal of land to defend, despite these natural advantages—the whole northern part of Manhattan Island. Colonel Robert Magaw, the officer in charge—both forts, as a unit, were the command of General Greene, who maintained his headquarters in Fort Lee across the river—had almost 3,000 men under him, too few to defend all the land, much too many to defend the fort itself, which was not meant to accommodate more than 1,000.

This "fort," the dominating site, the center of the defensive system, was no more than a five-pointed mud wall. It had no bastions. Because it rested on solid rock and the men who had built it had no experience with "blowing"—blasting—there was no ditch around it. Neither were there any casements or bombproofs. The fort embraced about four acres, and within it the only buildings were a set of offices and a magazine, both wooden. There were no barracks. The outworks were trifling—a few flèches, a few scattered redoubts, one of them only half finished.

Washington wavered. Outwardly imperturbable, as always, he was of several minds as to what he should do next—

or refrain from doing. Howe, he knew, now had upwards of 2,000 men immediately around him, for Percy had reinforced him because of the garrison replacements, and he had called in the late-coming Hessians from New Rochelle. On no account should he risk a rub with any considerable part of such an enemy.

What would Howe do next? Would he make one more attempt to trap and crush the Continental Army? Would he just go back to New York and call it a campaign? If he did that, would he pause to swamp Fort Washington on the way? Or would he, with more spirit than he usually showed, make a dash across New Jersey—all unprotected—and descend upon Philadelphia, which would fall like an overripe plum? The last was what Washington himself would have done, had he been in Howe's boots. To capture the two biggest cities in the American colonies, one of them, so to speak, the capital, would surely be to end the war. And the British, without question, wished to end this expensive war.

There was already an Army of the North as well as an Army of the South, concerning neither of which was Washington sure of his authority; and now, in his perplexity, his uncertainty, he split his own central army into no fewer than four parts. Greene had 3,500 men at forts Washington and Lee; Lee had almost 7,000 to watch Howe and to manoeuvre at will in Westchester County; and Heath was sent up to the Hudson Highlands, the West Point country, with 4,000 men and instructions to prevent the British from passing. Washington himself took only a few hundred men with him when he crossed the Hudson to New Jersey and set up headquarters at Hackensack. He expected to be greatly reinforced there by New Jersey militiamen, who would surely spring to the defense of their state. He was to be disappointed again.

In Hackensack he brooded about Fort Washington; and he had just about decided to go there and inspect the place for

The Tide Turns

himself, when a message arrived from the commanding officer, Colonel Magaw, by way of General Greene at Fort Lee. That morning, November 15, Magaw had been formally called upon to surrender the fort. The message—it was enclosed—contained a clause, customary at that time, pointing out the difficulty of controlling victory-maddened troops. Magaw took this seriously, as a threat that in case the British should storm the fort successfully everybody there would be put to the sword, and in his reply—a copy of which was also enclosed—he expressed sorrow that General Howe had permitted himself to play "a part so unworthy of himself and the British nation," which must have caused a chuckle in British headquarters. Magaw wrote, additionally—and here was another conventional, meaningless clause—that he would defend the fort to the last man.

Washington got on his horse and rode to Fort Lee. It was late at night when he arrived, and he learned that General Greene together with General Putnam were at the fort across the river for a last minute look-around. Washington started after them, in another boat, but met them coming back, and was so warmly assured by them that everything was fine at Fort Washington—the spirits of the men, the availability of supplies, Magaw's excellent dispositions, and all the rest—that he consented to return to Fort Lee and a bed. He was up before dawn, however, and he and Greene and Putnam and another general, Hugh Mercer, commander of the so-called Flying Camp of reserves in New Jersey, pushed off for the east bank.

Magaw had great faith in the ability of his fort—he thought of it as "his" because, together with Colonel Rufus Putnam the engineer (no relation to Old Put), he had supervised its construction—to hold out. A constant threat as a cover from which to sally, it would tie up a large part of the British Army, he contended. He would personally guarantee that it could be held against anything that the enemy could do, at least until the end of December.

There seemed to be no way in which they could help the optimistic colonel, except by getting out of his way. Four generals standing around doing nothing would not be good for the spirits of the men. The other three joined in urging Washington to return before the bombardment started, each declaring himself willing to remain if the commander-in-chief thought that Magaw might need the advice of a general officer. Washington did not think so; and they all went back across the Hudson. They were halfway over when they heard the British guns begin to boom.

Thereafter, and though they had spyglasses in their hands on the ramparts of Fort Lee, they followed the fight largely by ear. The artillery spoke for about two hours, and then, a little before ten, suddenly ceased. A splatter of musketry succeeded it on all sides of Mount Washington excepting the river side. The fire was answered with spirit from the various outposts of the fort. Here was no siege, which might take time, but an out-and-out assault. Howe, they had heard, was committing about 8,000 of his soldiery to it.

Gradually the sound of the guns became centered, drawing together. The outposts were being driven in. If they all had to take refuge at the fort itself—and it was beginning to sound that way—they'd be doomed, almost 3,000 men in a space meant for 1,000 at the most, and open to the sky. When the British brought up their fieldpieces the men behind those thick walls would be lost. And sure enough, once again the cannons, closer in, began to boom.

From Fort Lee they sent an officer across the river to beg Magaw to hold out until nightfall, when they believed that they could carry off his men: they had the boats.

The shooting, muskets and cannons alike, ceased. There was not even any more smoke.

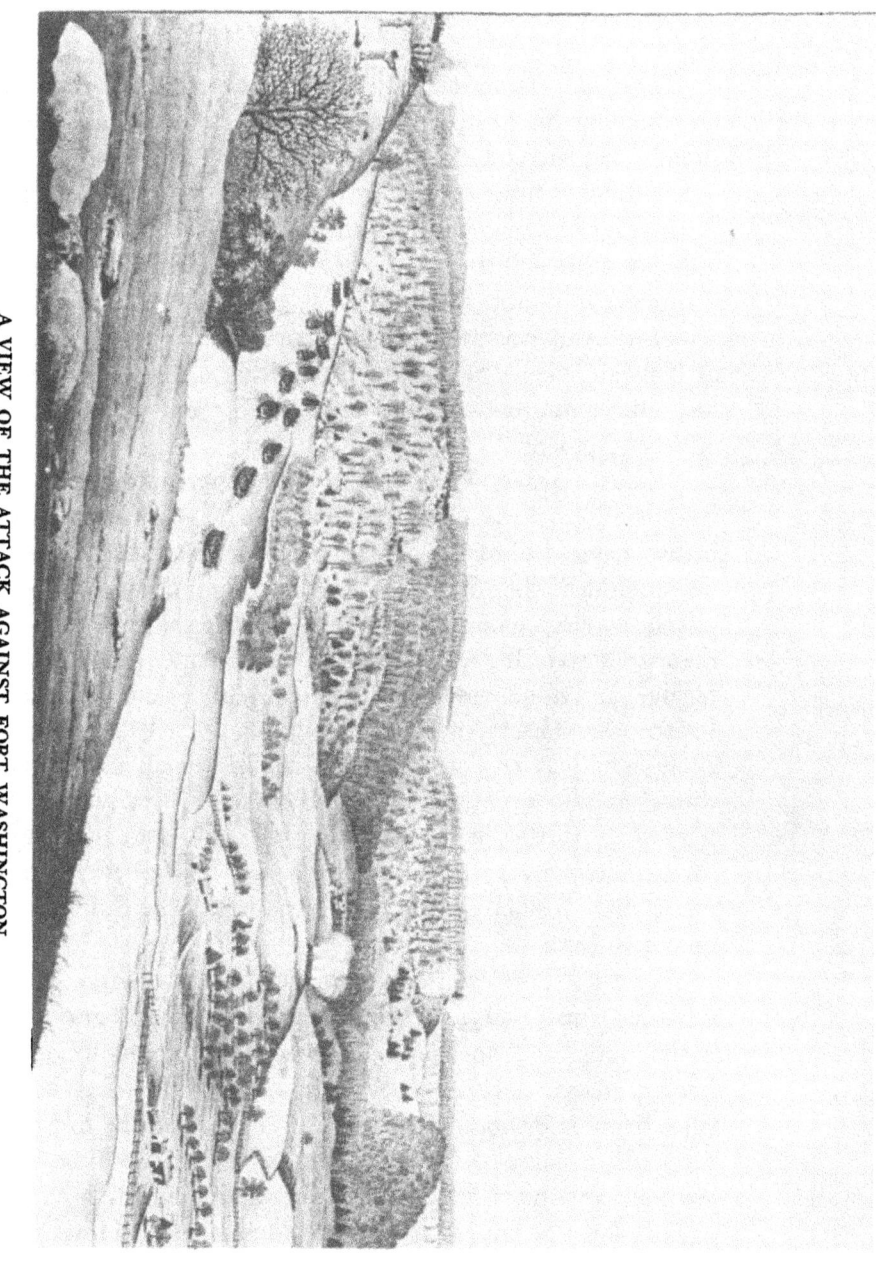

A VIEW OF THE ATTACK AGAINST FORT WASHINGTON

The officer-messenger, a young captain, returned. He was shaking his head. It was too late, he reported. Magaw already had surrendered.

That was three o'clock in the afternoon. It had taken the British and Hessians not until the end of December but only a little less than eight hours. They had been mauled, but the end was never in doubt.

The haul was stupendous: scores of cannons, hundreds of balls and shells, thousands of cartridges, tons of gunpowder, and tents, entrenching tools, food, and all manner of other equipment.

The prisoners numbered a little over 2,800, and they were the unluckiest of all. After they had run the gantlet of British camp followers—those accepted harridans whose duties included the doing of laundry and the insulting of prisoners—they would be chucked into noisome prison ships, there to starve. It was a system, if a vile one. Many did not survive, and none was ever the same again. The usual rake-off for the Commissary of Prisoners was 50 percent; but this one, a civilian, was especially avaricious and took almost two-thirds of the rations for himself, which is why the men starved. For this personage the fall of Fort Washington meant, literally, a fortune. And who was he? Why, none other than Joshua Loring, late of Boston, the Sultana's cooperative husband.

Charles Cornwallis, Earl Cornwallis, was a large, smooth, dignified man with a sleepy smile, amused gray eyes, a cleft chin, and one dead eye—the result of a collision in a hockey match at Eton many years before (the other lad had since become Bishop of Durham). In Parliament he had rather favored the cause of the American colonies, though he did so without any unmannerly enthusiasm; but when he fought against them he fought hard. He had no faith in Howe's dilatory methods. He believed that the way to move was fast. Four days after the fall of Fort Washington—why give the rebels a chance to see the light and clear out of Fort Lee bag and baggage?—Lord Cornwallis crossed the Hudson in two hundred boats to a point just below Dobb's Ferry. This was no hit-and-run raid. He had 6,000 men with him. A Tory—the thing had been well planned, despite the shortness of time—was waiting for them, ready to guide them up a little-known pass in the Palisades; and in a few hours they were marching, at a good clip, south toward Fort Lee, which was only six miles away.

It was not until then that Washington, in Hackensack, heard of it. He dashed to the scene.

There was no time to save any of the supplies. They did get out some of the precious gunpowder, but all of the guns would go to the British, and all of the tents (which were not even struck), all of the blankets, all of the entrenching tools. There were 1,000 barrels of flour, among other things. The very cooking kits were abandoned, the very food in the pots over the fires.

They were between two rivers, the British to the north of them in overwhelming numbers, Newark Bay to the south. There were no bridges over the Hudson, of course, and there was only one over the Hackensack. If they did not get to that one bridge before the British, they would be crushed, and once again—beyond the shadow of a doubt—the war would have been ended.

They got there. It was not a retreat; it was a flight.

The British took only 105 prisoners at Fort Lee, and these were men who in the excitement of clearing out had broken into the sutlers' rum supplies and were dead drunk. All the same, they would serve to swell Mr. Loring's take.

As for the men under Washington and Greene, a little

over 2,000 of them, they were again between two rivers, the Hackensack and the Passaic this time, on level ground, and they were hungry and cold and all their gear had been left behind.

It began to rain.

CHAPTER

11

Folks at the time knew what most persons since have never realized—that the War of the American Revolution was a *civil* war.[29] So many different tribes of redskins participated in so many different sectors of the frontier, and there were seen so many English, Scottish, Canadian, and German uniforms, and later so many that were French, and so determined too were the efforts to conduct the thing along European lines, that even at the time there might have been those who briefly forgot that it had started, after all, as a family fight. In the beginning there had been thousands of colonists who were neutral, not caring one way or the other; but there were districts where feeling was so strong that for all practical purposes the neutrals were forced in, were obliged to take sides. The main war, the acknowledged war, in the North and South and sometimes in the central states as well, was fringed by and often obstructed by a whole firework-spluttering of "little wars," some of which were no more than grudge fights while others were waged, and bitterly, on a large scale. Windows were smashed, barns and even houses were burned, men were threatened with tar and feathers—a hideous torture—

and battles and ambuscades were not rare. All war is a dirty business, but these "little wars" were the dirtiest.

New Jersey, far from the frontier, had been spared some of the most savage raids and massacres; but Whig-Tory fury, patriot-loyalist fury, flared as high there as anywhere else—and maybe higher.

The state had seemed, just at first, firmly in favor of independence, though there were pockets of Toryism reported, especially in Bergen and Monmouth counties. The Howe brothers, though, had reason to believe that many New Jerseyites were in secret loyal to King George and would come flocking to his colors as soon as the royal uniform was shown between Philadelphia and New York. The peace commissioners had confidence in New Jersey—or, as it was more often called, "the Jerseys."[30]

The response of the loyalists in Long Island and Westchester County, and in New York City itself, had been heartening, but at the same time a shade disconcerting. The loyalists had come in droves, true, but they were unorganized droves. For exact warfare these faithful ones expressed little love. The Howes had been allotted large supplies of weapons, mostly muskets, and of gunpowder and lead, for distribution among the American subjects who clung to their affiliation and were willing to fight for it; but most of the loyalists who applied for such handouts did not want them for the purpose of forming military companies, only for the purpose of taking occasional potshots at their Whig neighbors.

This the Howe brothers did not care for. An intensification of the brother-against-brother feeling, they saw, would only make the conflict harder to end; and in their role as carrot-holders they discouraged that. They announced that they would pass out arms only to such civilian subjects as had already organized themselves into companies and were willing to put their services at the disposal of the regular British mili-

The Tide Turns

tary authorities. There were many who did just that. Probably there were never more than 5,000 American loyalists under arms at any one time in the course of the Revolution, but considering the small territory that they had to draw on this was a good record. General Howe made some use of these troops, but not as fighters, only in garrison duty, transport, and the like. To have permitted them to fight against their fellow Americans would only have been to make his job as a contriver of peace that much harder.

For the same reason, his brother the Admiral flatly refused to issue letters of marque to the swarms of loyalist seamen who applied for them. The revolting colonies were dependent upon their Atlantic coastline for just about all of their supplies excepting food and timber—for guns, gunpowder, metal, cloth, everything—and the would-be privateers sought to prey on the heavy blockading traffic that had sprung up between the French West Indies and the Carolinas, contending that this would starve the rebels out. The Admiral said no. He was much criticized for this refusal, and always adversely, but he stuck to it. Internal dissension he did not want. Moreover, all regular navy men abhorred privateers, who made so much money without responsibility, and if Black Dick opened up privateering in those waters his desertion rate, scandalously high as it was, would soar.

Many of the loyalists were offended, even outraged; but the Brothers Howe persisted in their plan. They were stubborn, if sluggish, those two.

The last day of November they issued yet another proclamation, this one specifically addressed to the people of New Jersey, offering "protection papers" to all such as came in within the next sixty days and signed a disclaimer of all independency aims and a renewal of allegiance to King George. Any British officer could issue these, and they cost nothing.

The move was a shrewd one. The Jerseys already had

been invaded, and no doubt soon would be overrun, south and north, east and west, for what could that contemptible little Continental Army do to prevent it? Here was rich farming country, like Long Island, like Westchester. Rumors of how the redcoats and Hessians, especially the Hessians, had behaved in those other two places must already have seeped down to the Jerseys, where there would be consternation. Soon after landing on Staten Island, Howe had issued a general order to the troops under his command that anybody caught looting would be shot. He seemed to have forgotten this. He did issue a couple of further orders along those lines, but they were progressively weaker. And nobody ever was shot or hanged or flogged or otherwise punished, in that army, for stealing from civilians.

The Hessians were probably to blame. Looting by soldiers was an accepted practice in Europe, and they had been told on the way across the Atlantic that they could make their fortunes among the Americans, whose homes bulged with riches. Moreover, those same Americans were rebels against their king, their rightful master, and so deserved no mercy. Even the officers among the Hessians believed this. None of them ever displayed the slightest interest in the American cause for independence. They *assumed* that it was wicked. Hence, they did nothing to restrain their men, and indeed they not infrequently participated in the plundering when the loot promised to glitter. As for the soldiers, they simply crammed their arms with all that they could carry, and when there was more than that they stole horses to carry it for them. They were like a horde of devastating ants. They were impersonal—and they left almost nothing behind.

With such an example before them—and the redcoats, no angels themselves, did not like the Hessians, a feeling that was reciprocated—how could the British officers restrain *their* men? It is not a matter of record that they tried very hard.

In New Jersey it would be different, the Howes hoped. This clearly was the purpose of the protection papers, and possession of such a paper would exempt an otherwise defenseless man from pillage. It said that right on the papers themselves, didn't it? It said that they were "For the Protection of Inhabitants and their Property." That sounded fine. Hundreds began to sign up.

There will always be men like this, me-tooers who beam right and left on each side alternatively and will swear to anything; but when fear or trickery or a desire to protect loved ones resulted in the signatures of such hitherto staunch patriots as John Covenhoven, Judge Samuel Tucker, and Richard Stockton (a signer of the Declaration of Independence!) the business looked serious indeed.

George Washington at first was too busy trying to keep his army intact to pay much attention.

He had crossed the Passaic River at Aquackanock[31] on November 21, and the following day he was in Newark, where he rested for five days, while he sent in all directions appeals for more recruits. He knew, however, that Cornwallis was close behind him, and for all the rain Lord Cornwallis was not a man to dawdle.

Lord Stirling had been exchanged for a royal governor, Mountfort Browne, of the Bahamas, and Sullivan had been exchanged for Brigadier General Richard Prescott, whom Montgomery had taken at Montreal. Sullivan was now with General Lee, as his second-in-command, while Stirling led a few hundred men, as ragged, as hungry, and as wet as Washington's own, in and around New Brunswick on the Raritan River. Staten Island is opposite, and with his control of that island and the surrounding waters General Howe could have penetrated middle New Jersey and cut Washington off from the south while Cornwallis was descending upon him from the north. It did not even seem to have occurred to Howe to do this, but Washington could not take the chance: he had to concentrate his badly scattered forces. He joined Stirling at New Brunswick. He wrote to Lee to suggest that he cross to the Jerseys and join him, the commander-in-chief.

As for Howe, he had no need to draw in his forces. On the contrary, at this time he was sending *his* second-in-command, General Henry Clinton, to Newport, Rhode Island, with some 6,000 men. It is hard to see why he did this. Newport—and as a by-product, Providence—did guarantee control not only of Narragansett Bay but also of the eastern end of Long Island Sound, a favorite scooting-through place for blockade runners; but the navy and a few Marines could have accomplished the same end. As it was, the soldiers simply stayed there for three years, doing nothing.[32] It can only be assumed that Howe could not stand the sight of Clinton around headquarters any longer.

On the last day of the month, the very day that the Howes issued their proclamation, Washington pleaded with the New Jersey and Maryland militia brigades to stay a little longer, though their enlistment term was up. They refused; and they marched out of New Brunswick, 2,000 of them, as Cornwallis with his pursuing 6,000 were approaching the town a few miles away.

Washington started for Princeton.

Stirling's men had to burn their tents before they left New Brunswick, for they had no wagons in which to carry them. It broke their hearts to do this—also, it was a hard job, what with the rain—but they did it. Then they marched after Washington.

Washington did not stop long at Princeton, but he left orders for Stirling to stay there. The commander-in-chief himself pushed on to Trenton. He could see that to avert annihilation he must immediately put the Delaware between his men and the enemy, and he had sent west one Colonel

Richard Humpton in command of a small body of men who scoured both banks of the river for some seventy miles north of Philadelphia, seizing all boats as a matter of military necessity. They were thorough, these men. They missed nothing. When Washington reached Trenton he found their whole nautical bag waiting for him. He transported his sick and his baggage first, and soon he got all of his men over as well.

Meanwhile, Stirling and *his* men were comfortable for the first time in many days, for they had holed up in the deserted college building at Princeton. They feared, though, that they could expect Cornwallis at any moment.

Cornwallis did not come as soon as that. He loitered for four days at New Brunswick, though he knew that he had been close behind the Continentals: his advance guard had exchanged shots with their rear guard. Cornwallis had asked to be allowed to pursue Washington beyond New Brunswick, which was as far as his orders took him, but this had been denied, Howe telling him to remain there until he, Howe, joined him. This was the reason for the four-day delay, four mighty important days in American history.

On the west bank of the Delaware, Washington did get a few reinforcements—the Philadelphia Associators, a volunteer group, and German companies from Maryland and Pennsylvania. He then had about 1,200 men. Stirling had an equal number, at Princeton.

Washington crossed the Delaware again, to the east bank, thinking that he might do something to help Stirling, but he met that sturdy Scot in full retreat midway between Trenton and Princeton. Howe had appeared in New Brunswick, and, seeing the situation, had released Cornwallis, who was making for Princeton with all possible haste, in the company of his commanding officer.

Washington turned around and went back, with Stirling. Their last boats were still in midstream when the British entered Trenton. Howe ordered Cornwallis to go north along the river, Von Donop south, in search of boats. They found none. Washington had taken them all. That satisfied the Baroness von Kielmannsegge's grandson, who thereupon ordered his men, British and Hessians alike, into a series of winter stations—New Brunswick, Pennington, Trenton, Bordentown—and himself started back for New York and the charms of La Loring. As far as *he* was concerned the campaign of 1776 was over.

George Washington had different ideas.

CHAPTER

12

O<small>N THE DAY</small> of the evacuation of Fort Lee, Washington had caused an aide to write to the general after whom that base had been named, and the next day, with a little more time, he wrote to Lee himself, in his own hand. Each of these letters expressed the wish that Lee march from White Plains into and across New Jersey and join his army with Washington's. These were not commands, only strong suggestions. Whether from natural politeness or because of some lingering traces of awe of Charles Lee, the commander-in-chief refrained from giving peremptory orders.

When Lee consented to reply it was with blurred, hazy excuses. His force had been much reduced a little while ago when the Massachusetts militia walked out on him. Many of those left were on the sick list. His men did not have enough clothes and neither did they have enough shoes for such a march. Instead, he wrote to General Heath at the Highlands headquarters, ordering him—on what authority it would be hard to say—to detach two of his own brigades and send them to Washington. This Heath refused to do. Heath pointed out that he had been instructed by the commander-in-chief to hold the Highlands Hudson pass at all costs, and that the loss of two brigades would cripple him. Baffled, Lee at last consented to go—but he went at a snail's pace. More, he was overtaken when in northern New Jersey by the remnants of seven regiments, about 500 men, sent by Gates from the Army of the North to Washington at the commander-in-chief's own request, and he annexed these units to his own army, so that thereafter they too moved at a snail's pace.

Washington wrote again on December 10, *entreating* him to hasten, and to this Lee languidly replied that he might be of more help to the Continental cause here on the flanks of the enemy instead of placing himself, with Washington, before them. He had a condescending manner now, like one who patiently explains the obvious to a nitwit. He was treating Washington like an overzealous and impetuous youngster; and in fact he *was* older than the commander-in-chief—by exactly sixteen days![33]

From letters that Lee wrote to others, and in particular to Colonel Reed of Washington's staff and his fellow British Army officer Horatio Gates, commander of the Army of the North, it is plain that he thought Philadelphia and the main Continental Army were doomed. He had no wish to take a part in that demise. If he could loaf diligently enough he might survive it as the head of an independent command still in the field. And who could tell what might happen then? He might accomplish some brilliant stroke that would cause the Howes to treat with him when they sued for peace. He could thus end up as the savior of his adopted country. He had confidence if he had nothing else, did Charles Lee. When people hailed him as a genius he agreed.

Lee was not the only one who believed that Philadelphia was about to fall. That city itself bordered on a state of panic, and every Whig with friends or relatives living in the country was getting out of town with as many of his goods as he could tote. Military supplies were shifted south, into Delaware. Congress, right after it had vehemently denied reports that it was about to fly to Baltimore, flew to Baltimore.

This wonder-city of Philadelphia, largest in America, third largest after London and Bristol in the whole English-speaking world, this City of Brotherly Love, with its Philosophical Society, its famous Christ Church steeple, its State House, its full mile of waterfront and many miles of straight streets, some of them paved, this city of 38,000 population had no regular garrison and no fortifications save the river blockade—and the experience of New York had proved that underwater obstacles were of limited value. Its only defenders, aside from what citizens remained—and three out of four houses were empty—were Washington's scarecrows, a few thousand of them, strewn along the river for a stretch of about twenty miles. Would *they* ever serve to stop the British when the British decided to cross? It was unlikely.

It was true that all the boats were on the Pennsylvania side, and true too that the British apparently had brought no pontoons with them. But they could send back to New York for pontoons, couldn't they? And they could build boats. There were wooden houses that could be pulled apart. There were carpenters whose services could be coerced. And in the village of Trenton alone there were three blacksmiths.

Anyway, if the winter proved as cold as it now threatened, the Delaware would soon be frozen over thick enough to support the British, heavy guns and all.

There was one faint note of hopefulness. The incorrigible Tom Paine had traveled with the army across New Jersey as a common soldier, but his duties as such could not have been very onerous, for he found time to write another best-seller. Started in Newark, this was finished in Philadelphia, and rushed to the printers. Following the sensational success of Paine's first book, *Common Sense*, it was seized as fast as the presses could turn it out. It was called *The Crisis*, and it opened with some memorable words:

> These are the times that try men's souls: The summer soldier and the sunshine patriot will, in this crisis, shrink from the service of his country; but he that stands it Now, deserves the love and thanks of man and woman. Tyranny, like hell, is not easily conquered; yet we have this consolation with us, that the harder the conflict, the more glorious the triumph.

It was read before the soldiers, in small groups.

In such a state of confusion, not to say anarchy, was Philadelphia that it was deemed necessary to proclaim martial law, and Old Put was made military governor. He promptly issued a statement denying that the high command had any intention of abandoning the city. The city would be defended to the last man, he declared. Nobody believed this.

The weather continued raw and rainy. Sickness among the exposed troops was rampant, and doctors were more difficult than ever to get. The situation in New Jersey appeared to be worsening every day. The legislature was breaking up, its members perparing to deny that they had ever served. It was reported that almost two thousand Jerseyites already had signed "protection papers," and they were still flocking in. Why not? New Jersey had seen a sad and seedy army marching the wrong way. That retreat from Hackensack, as one grim observer put it, "made thousands of Tories."

Darkest of all loomed the terrible date, January 1, 1777. On that day the enlistment terms of a great majority of those under arms would expire, and it was certain that almost none of the men would re-enlist. The Continental Army, then, would cease to exist.

The Continental cause needed a resounding success, but how could it get such a thing? There was gloom at headquarters. Washington maintained his statue-like immobility, but even he was writing to his nephew: "I think the game is pretty near up.[34]

He wrote to Lee again December 10 and yet again December 14, when, with just a touch of acerbity, he contended that although an army on the flanks of the enemy might well be effective, as Lee had graciously pointed out, it would not be so if there was no army *before* the enemy.

He might have saved himself the trouble. The first letter had no effect on the lagging lieutenant; the second never reached him. A few hours after Washington had written and sent the second letter he heard of the curious fate that had overtaken his second-in-command.

Washington by this time had developed a reasonably effective spy system. Congress had granted him a secret hoard of gold coins for this purpose, and he made good use of these. Not all of the residents of New Jersey had suddenly become sympathetic with the royal cause, and indeed the protection papers, after the first flush of success, had kicked back into the teeth of their issuers. The redcoats ignored them, and the Hessians, the worst offenders, couldn't read them; so that even a Tory Philadelphian, Joseph Stansbury, scolded General Howe in print for

> *This magical Mantle o'er Property thrown,*
> *Secur'd it from all sorts of Thieves—but his own!*

Washington, then, knew where Lee was. He was in Morris County, breezing along toward the Delaware at the rate of three miles a day. Cornwallis, at Pennington (which he, like Washington, always spelled "Penny Town"), did not. Cornwallis, worried about his wife, who was seriously ill, and eager to get settled in winter quarters so that he could go back to England and be with her, worried also about Lee, and quite as much as did Washington, though for a different reason.

Damn it, Lee was a real soldier, and it was not safe to have such a man near you and not be informed as to his strength and exact position. Had not Lee been a lieutenant colonel in the British Army? Hadn't he led Burgoyne's 16th Light Horse to glory in Portugal, and did not Cornwallis have that same regiment with him right here at Pennington? (Burgoyne was in Canada, but it was not customary in the British Army at that time for colonels to lead their own regiments in the field: they just *owned* the regiments, which were led by the lieutenant colonels.) It did not seem at all ironic when Cornwallis called for volunteers to scout out Lee and to report his presence, and if possible his strength, that one of those who stepped forward was the present active head of the 16th Light Horse, Lieutenant Colonel William Harcourt, a younger brother of Earl Harcourt. This lad got the job. He took thirty picked troopers with him, and three other young officers went along just for the fun of it.[35]

This would be no picnic! As the disillusionment had set in, it had got so that in no part of New Jersey was a single Britisher or Hessian, or even a small party, safe. Farmers, who resented being robbed, had formed a habit of firing at them from behind trees or from ditches. And Morris County, still with its wooded hills a hotbed of rebels, was the most perilous place of all.

Lee spent three days in Morristown, and then, November 13, he drifted over to Vealton—a long jump for him, eight miles. He did not himself stay in the Vealton camp, which he left in charge of General Sullivan, but with his own aides, his bodyguard, and a couple of newly arrived French volunteer officers pushed on about three miles to Basking Ridge and the Widow White's tavern.

Why Lee did this is one of history's mysteries. It was not a habit of his. He might have had paper work to do, but this could have been done at least as conveniently in camp. The

THE WIDOW WHITE'S TAVERN AT BASKING RIDGE, WHERE GENERAL CHARLES LEE WAS CAPTURED

Widow White was not, nor did she have, a celebrated cook, nor yet did she boast a large wine cellar.

A woman? This is possible, and it was so whispered, but such whispers were inevitable, and there was no evidence to support them. It would not be like Lee to desire to get away from the camp routine for a little while, for in fact he rather fancied himself as a "soldiers' soldier," and gloried in the hardships of outdoor life.

At any rate, there he went, and there he slept, and in the morning, seated in a dressing robe, he wrote a letter to his friend General Gates. It was a letter that reeked of vanity, boastful even as Lee's letters went, and in it he castigated Washington (without naming him) as "damnably deficient." He had just finished this letter—it was about ten o'clock—

when Harcourt's men came galloping up the lane and shot out the windows of the tavern.

It had been a stroke of luck on their part, not any plan. Roaming, aimless, they had come upon and questioned a messenger who was headed for the Widow White's with dispatches for the General, and they went there in his stead. They were deep in enemy territory, only a few miles from an army that might be expected to keep in touch with its commanding officer. They knew that they would have to move fast; and move fast they did.

It had turned very cold in the night, a hard frost, and the members of the General's bodyguard were either looking for firewood or else behind the stable trying to keep out of the wind and in the sun at the same time. They were quickly routed. The British horsemen called that if General Lee did not surrender right away they would burn the building down.

There was a great deal of confusion but no real resistance. Meekly, and in a matter of minutes, Charles Lee came out of the front door, his sword in his hands. The sword was taken from him; he was heaved, dressing robe and all, onto a spare horse; and the party galloped away.

Nobody else had been touched, or even cursed. Nothing had been stolen—excepting, of course, one major general.

CHAPTER

13

HISTORIANS have whooped, perhaps somewhat over-exuberantly, that the capture of Charles Lee was the best thing that ever happened to the Continental cause. At the time it was not so regarded. A shock, it was looked upon as a tragedy almost as great as the loss of Fort Washington. Who now would guide the American arms? The man might have been slightly mad, or at the age of forty-four prematurely senile, but by everybody's admission, including his own, he did know a great deal about the Military Art, which was more than could be said about anybody else on the colonists' side.

The British were jubilant. King George thanked Harcourt personally. The uprising would now collapse, they crowed. Nor were they gentle with their distinguished prisoner. They kept him in close confinement for more than half a year before they consented to accept his parole, though a parole for a man of his rank was customary—all but mandatory—at the time. There was even some talk of hanging Lee. He had resigned his British Army commission before accepting a commission in the Continental Army, true, but the resignation had not been *accepted* at that time, and so, it was argued, he was technically guilty of treason. Besides, once a British Army officer always a British Army officer, wasn't that true? Nobody seemed to know what to do about this.

All unabashed, Lee himself, deprived temporarily of the chance to tell George Washington how he should run his campaign, proceeded to tell William Howe, and at great length, how *he* should run *his*. This extraordinary document, which among other things recommends a force of some 4,000 to be stationed in Maryland and Delaware for the purpose of cutting communications between North and South, as well as a naval rather than an overland approach to Philadelphia, might have been read by the Howes; but assuredly it did little to affect the war.[36]

Whatever Washington's real feeling about the loss of Lee might have been, *immediately* it meant that he was at last to get that army he craved. General Sullivan, succeeding to the command at Vealton, sent out a rescue party as soon as he heard what had happened at the Widow White's tavern. It was too late. Harcourt and his light-horse party did not return by the way they had come, for they were warned that the countryside along that route was up in arms against them, but instead took a longer way back to Pennington, so that the would-be rescuers missed them.

Sullivan then did what Washington would have wished him to do. He proceeded to put the army on the march for the Delaware. He arrived in Washington's camp north of Philadelphia on December 20, in a raging snowstorm.

They were a woebegone lot, tatterdemalions. They shivered, and some could barely stand. Lee had at various times reported them to number 5,000, 4,000, and 3,000. In fact, they proved to number a bare 2,000, leaving out Gates's men, so many of their sick had been left behind. Yet many of these men were, in effect, veterans. They were that rarity in the Continental Army, soldiers who had been under fire.

With these tottering ragamuffins, and with his original whittled-down force, and such scanty reinforcements as he had been able to get locally—a total of about 7,500 men—Washington proposed to mount a counteroffensive.

What else could he do? There were only eleven days before the end of the enlistment period, after which, he calculated, he would have about 1,400 or 1,500 men left, not enough to wage even irregular warfare. He must strike while he still had something to strike with.

Spies had brought to the Continental headquarters Howe's order directing the taking up of winter quarters, an order issued December 13, the same day that Lee was captured, and Howe himself, on the 16th, had returned to New York. In Washington's camp few believed this. It was not that they questioned the information supplied by the spies, but only that they could not conceive of any general stopping for the winter so near to such a desirable goal. It didn't make sense. Besides, the Continental leaders had steeled themselves to expect the worst. They *had* to act as if they thought that this was just a trick.

Running the war on the British side, the Howes' immediate boss, was the secretary of state for the colonies, one Lord George Germain, who under an earlier name and title of Lord George Sackville had refused to order a charge of the British cavalry at the Battle of Minden, assumedly because he just didn't like the commander-in-chief, Prince Ferdinand of Brunswick—a refusal that turned what should have been a glorious victory into an indecisive standoff. For this refusal a court-martial found him guilty not of cowardice but of deliberate and willful disobedience, and decreed that he was "unfit to serve his Majesty in any military capacity whatever." Here was an odd one to be conducting a war, especially a war in a country he knew nothing about. There were general officers in the British Army who would have refused to serve under

Germain, for they esteemed him a disgrace to the service; but it would seem that the Howes did not feel that way.

"The chain, I own, is rather too extensive," William Howe reported to Germain after his return to New York. He went on to explain that the people of New Jersey were generally well favored to the royal cause, and that they needed the soldiers near them to protect them from vengeful Whigs. He thought that he should hold on to New Jersey all that winter.

He did not add, what he must have thought, that in all probability Washington's rabble would simply disintegrate and blow away before the following spring, and that it would be easy then for the British to take over Philadelphia and thus split the colonies in half.

The "chain" consisted of posts extending from Amboy at the mouth of the Raritan through New Brunswick, Princeton, Pennington, Trenton, and Bordentown. Howe had first meant it to stretch even farther, to Burlington, below Bordentown on the Delaware River, but Commodore Thomas Seymour, who had charge of all the American vessels, gondolas, and row-galleries above the chevaux-de-frise at Billingsport and below the falls at Trenton, roundly declared that he would burn the town by means of red-hot projectiles if he saw a single redcoat or Hessian there; so *that* plan was dropped.

The lower part of this line—in military parlance, the left wing—Trenton and Bordentown, was occupied almost entirely by Hessians. This might seem odd, for it was of course the most perilous post, since it was the nearest to the rebel force. Traditionally, so far in this war, the Hessians had held the left wing. To replace them now might seem to impugn their military "honor," about which they were touchy; and there was enough hard feeling as it was; so Howe allowed them to stay there.

The weakest link in the "chain," as it was the nearest to the main Continental camp, was Trenton. It was a pretty little village at the highest navigable point on the river, of about one hundred scattered houses, most of them wooden, and two principal streets, Queen and King,[37] besides a few numbered cross streets and a Front Street. It had no natural, geographical defenses excepting the Delaware on one side, which could be crossed by a ferry at this point but because of its width was readily defendable, and the Assunpink Creek on the south, bridged in the town and fordable a little farther up.

The town was garrisoned by slightly over 1,500 men, all, excepting 20 British light dragoons, Hessians. They comprised 50 jägers, and three regiments, crack outfits each of them: the Ralls in dark blue, the Lossbergs in scarlet, and the Knyphausen fusiliers in black, a polychromatic lot. They were headed by a red-faced, nail-chewing colonel named Johann Gottlieb von Rall, who refused to build fortification even when commanded to do so by his superior, Brigadier General von Donop. When his own second-in-command, Major Dechow, urged him to dig trenches as outworks, Von Rall cried: *"Lasst sie nur kommen! Keine Schanzen! Mit dem Bajonet wollen wir an sie!"*[38] He had a very low opinion of Americans as soldiers. He was to change this opinion.

In nearby Bordentown, under Von Donop, there were stationed three battalions of Hessian grenadiers, one company of jägers, one company of British light infantry, and the whole British 42nd regiment, the Black Watch. They were not all in the town. Some were at outposts in Mansfield Square and Black Horse Tavern.[39]

The nearest post in the other direction, north, was Pennington, with an all-British garrison. Lord Cornwallis was no longer there: he was in New York, packing and otherwise preparing to go home to his sick wife.

CHAPTER

14

ON A CHILL MORNING late in December, a Ranger foraging party of the sort that was forever harassing the Hessians with hit-and-run raids crossed from the east to the west banks of the Delaware with, among other prizes, a prisoner. This was John Honeyman, according to the Rangers a notorious Tory. They had caught him skulking near Trenton, in suspicious circumstances, and they believed him to be a spy. Anyway, they were taking no chances. When they rode into the Continental camp they had Honeyman's wrists tied behind him, his ankles lashed under the belly of his horse.

Any matter even remotely related to spying must be turned over to the commander-in-chief: that was a standing order. Nevertheless, the Rangers were astounded when General Washington did indeed take charge of this case personally. While all the camp marveled, the commander-in-chief was closeted with John Honeyman for almost an hour, alone, all secretaries and aides having been turned out-of-doors. Afterward, Washington confirmed the arrest and ordered that Honeyman be jailed for trial by a military court in the morning. The man was jailed all right, but he was never tried. He wasn't there in the morning. Somebody—on orders from the commander-in-chief?—had left a door open.

George Washington had not had much military experience—none at all in any regular army, only with the militia—when he took command of the new Continental forces in the field before Boston in 1775, just after the Battle of Bunker Hill. As was only natural, he tended at first to try to do too much on his own, not from bossiness but because he was so conscientious. He soon learned better. Increasingly, as the war continued and as his own staff grew larger and more efficient, he learned to delegate authority, as any good executive must.

In one category, however, the General would accept no assistance. He did all the spy-directing himself. He was a man who could keep his mouth shut brilliantly. He had a small chest, which only he was permitted even to approach, and it contained gold guineas secretly granted to him by Congress. At one time he was believed to have had as many as 1,800 of these, a fortune.

Spies, like dispatch riders, demanded cash. Continental paper money might be fobbed off by the bushel basketful to drovers and sutlers, bakers and farmers, but the dispatch riders and the secret agents, mindful of the perils of their professions, insisted upon being paid in metal, not this new paper stuff.

Spies insisted, additionally, that when the war was over, or when their own particular parts in it were over, their friends and neighbors should be officially notified that the Tory pose had never been anything but that, a trick employed to gain Tory confidence and Tory information. This was done so that they could live in peace afterward, without fear of a belated tar-and-feathers or rail-riding party. Every spy that Washington hired had made this demand; and in each case he had acquiesced; and in each case, too, he had lived up to his promise.[40]

Honeyman, a veteran of Quebec under Wolfe, *was* a spy—for the Continental cause. He had contrived to get himself branded as an anti-independence man, and posing as a dealer in cattle he had been in and out of Trenton several times, always with his eyes wide open.

Washington was particularly interested in Trenton. Of the various links in the chain of posts the British had stretched across New Jersey, Trenton, Washington now knew, was the weakest. It was also the nearest. Trenton, he decreed, was doomed.

For he had decided to take the offensive. What else could he do? Once the Delaware was frozen—and this could happen any night now—the British could cross in crushing force. Washington could not protect Philadelphia, the capital of the country. What little remained of the so-called "Grand Army" would dissolve in a week or so, when enlistments ran out. He could not sit still. He could not retreat. He had to attack.

This was generally understood around headquarters, but the utmost secrecy was enforced. All leaves were canceled. The men were instructed to prepare three days of cooked rations. Boats were being massed along the west shore. The field officers, alerted, knew that *something* spectacular was about to happen, but only a few of the very highest among them knew what it was.

The details were announced at a last-minute council of war, Christmas Eve, at Washington's headquarters, William Keith's comfortable house on Knowles's Creek a few miles from Newtown. There were present at this momentous conclave major generals Sullivan and Greene, brigadiers Stirling, De Fermoy, Mercer, Stephen, and St. Clair, and colonels Sargent, Knox, Stark, and Glover; also, of course, the commander-in-chief; and also, inexplicably, the Reverend Doctor Alexander Macwhorter, a Presbyterian from Newark, who, assumedly, called for divine guidance of the venture.

Washington meant to gamble every man he had; yet his plan, though bold, could hardly be called simple. It called for a four-pronged attack, no less, across the Delaware.

Israel Putnam, a major general who did not attend the Keith House conference, being too busy with his duties as military governor of Philadelphia, had been expected to take across as many militiamen as he could spare; but Old Put, for once, was not filled with fire, and he mumbled excuses, so that it looked as if he would not cross at all—or at least, only if conditions were perfect. Putnam, the men at headquarters were saying, had lost his fighting edge.

General James Ewing had about 1,000 Pennsylvania and New Jersey militiamen posted along the river from Yardley's Ferry to Bond's Ferry, which plied to Bordentown. Ewing was assigned to cross the river on Christmas Day, landing to the south of Trenton, and to man the bridge over Assunpink Creek, thus preventing a retreat to or a reinforcement from Bordentown, some six miles to the south.

The most southerly Continental post was at and around Bristol, where about 1,800 men were under the command of John Cadwalader, senior colonel of the Philadelphia Associators, a silk-stocking group drawn largely from Philadelphia. His assignment was to hit Bordentown and keep Von Donop and the Hessians and Highlanders busy there, so that they would not be able to go to the assistance of those who faced the main attack at Trenton. General Horatio Gates was in Philadelphia, and Washington had been pleading with him to take command of this southernmost force, in part because the commander-in-chief feared that the men would refuse to follow a mere colonel, even so energetic a one as Cadwalader. Gates, however, was being coy. He wished to go to Baltimore and do some politicking among the self-exiled members of Congress. It was widely rumored that he was eying Washington's post.[41]

The main part of the army, about 2,400 men in two divisions under Sullivan and Greene, with Washington in overall command, would cross the Delaware at McKonkey's Ferry, about nine miles north of Trenton,[42] which town they would attack from the north.

All of this was to take place the following night—the night of December 25–26, 1776.

Much depended upon the weather, which was very cold. The river had not frozen near Trenton and Philadelphia, but it had frozen up north, and already from that direction great chunks of ice were floating. These were mostly along the shores, not in the middle of the stream, but they might make the handling of the boats at both shores a ticklish business. John Glover of Marblehead promised that his boys would take care of that, and the commander-in-chief nodded, satisfied.

So—everything was ready.

Chapter

15

Putnam did not budge.

Ewing, in the middle station, never got off the bank. He took one look at an ice-clogged river and assumed that the commander-in-chief would postpone the trip. That is what any sensible man would do. It's what *he* did.

As Washington was about to mount his horse and start for the rendezvous at McKonkey's Ferry that raw Christmas day, James Wilkinson, a brash young aide of General Gates, rode up and presented him with a communication.

"What a time is this to hand me letters," Washington fumed.

Wilkinson apologized but said that he had been instructed to do so by General Gates.

"By General Gates? Where is he?"

"I left him this morning in Philadelphia."

"What was he doing there?"

"I understood him that he was on his way to Congress."

"On his way to Congress!"

And Washington broke the seal and read the letter. He made no comment, only nodding a dismissal.[43]

So the General preferred not to make himself available? He probably had little faith in the enterprise. Washington sighed, and sat down to write an urgent message to Cadwalader, begging him to land at least *some* of his men and make at least *some* sort of diversion.

Cadwalader tried: that much must be said for him. He tried hard, and for many hours; but the high water, the current, and the ice floes were too much for him. He did manage to land some of his men near Bordentown, but he could not get his guns ashore. Anyway, he reasoned, Washington, despite his note of that morning—it was a Wednesday— would certainly postpone the venture. And then he, Cadwalader, with only part of his force and with no guns, would be trapped in New Jersey, faced with the Hessians and Highlanders from both Bordentown and Trenton, and unable to expect any relief. He assumed, as Ewing had, that Washington, even if he tried, could never make it to the New Jersey side. So he went back to Pennsylvania.

The lower Deleware was for practical purposes divided into two parts—above and below the Falls of Trenton. Philadelphia, Bristol, and Bordentown were below the Falls, where the river was wider and deeper, the current trickier. Conditions below the Falls that Christmas night were admittedly bad, as bad as anybody could remember having seen them. They were bad enough *above* the Falls, where the floating ice presented a problem even to such tried-and-true boat-handlers as John Glover's men from Marblehead; yet Washington never even gave a thought to the possibility of turning back.

It was a night of full moon, though the moon seldom was seen, for the clouds were low and thick. It was a glowering wet night, cold, and the wind was from the northeast.

The river at McKonkey's Ferry was a little less than 1,000 feet across. There was almost no ice in the middle, but

The Tide Turns

the banks were cluttered with it. The stuff kept piling on top of itself, squeeing hideously.

The men had been paraded that afternoon on a flat plain behind hills that screened them from possibly peering eyes on the east bank. Soon after sundown they began to appear at the river's edge, in small groups, each man carrying a blanket, rations for three days, 400 rounds of ammunition, and some extra flints. The flints in the Continental Army were good—much better than those the British had—but even so, and even if it was possible to keep the powder dry, the lock mechanism or the priming pan might get wet, in which case the gun would be no good except as a club or as a thing on which to mount a bayonet—if you had a bayonet. The men had been warned to wrap their flintlocks in some kind of cloth, though too many of them needed whatever cloth they might possess for their feet, which often were bare and bleeding.

Below the Falls the leaders were supposed to ship men and guns aboard any sort of rowboats, sailboats, or barges that were available, even, if these might do the trick, aboard rafts. Above the Falls there was never any question about the nature of the vehicles. They would be Durham boats.

These, the invention of Robert Durham, were designed for upper-river traffic, and they had been in use for many years, transporting 15 to 20 tons of flour, corn, wheat, iron, and whisky down from New York and the northern parts of New Jersey and Pennsylvania, 2 to 3 tons of manufactured goods back. A Durham boat ran from 40 to 66 feet in length, 8 feet in beam, and drew, not loaded, only about 2 feet. The crew customarily consisted of five, including the steersman, who was also the skipper. The boat was double-ended, somewhat like a huge canoe, and had a keel. It could be rowed, but most of the time it was poled, the upper river being in general shallow; and the polers, grasping 20-foot sticks, walked runways that ran from stem to stern. Stem and stern on a

Durham were the same anyway, and the sweep by means of which the boat was steered could be fitted into either end. There was also a mast from which two sails could be spread when the wind was right. There were about forty of these vessels in the upper Delaware, and Washington, who had been assembling them for some time, had most of them for his crossing.[44] They had been massed, amid stern secrecy, mostly at night, behind heavily wooded Malta Island, close to the west bank near the mouth of Knowles's Creek. Bringing them to the McKonkey's Ferry landing after dark was a major labor. This, again, was because of the ice. The boats rode high, the water was shallow, so that the men, quiet and well-behaved, if needs be could wade out, holding their muskets above their heads; and many of them at least were to land that way; but with the fieldpieces and the ammunition wagons, not to mention the horses told off to haul both, it was different. The boats had to be brought right alongside for *this* cargo.

The army was provided with eighteen fieldpieces, nine for each division—six 6-pounders, seven 3-pounders, three 4-pounders, and two 5.5-inch howitzers. Here was a startling departure from the military practice of the time. Since the days of Marlborough, the better part of a century back, a properly equipped army was expected to have from two to three cannons for every 1,000 infantrymen. This force of about 2,400, it will be seen, carried three times that many. Why?

There were several reasons.

A cannon would shoot farther. A musket was ineffective beyond one hundred yards; a rifle would reach three hundred yards but could not be fitted with a bayonet; a cannon could kill at five hundred yards with solid balls, better than half that distance if shotted with grape or canister.

It was not raining when the men first assembled, but the

The Tide Turns

air was sodden, sullen, threatening. Muskets could not be fired if the locks or the priming powder were wet—or even damp. The same applied to rifles. Cannons, however, were plugged against moisture. Their powder was carried in waterproof containers, more immediately in showerproof bags of oiled silk. The cannons were not set off by means of a sparking apparatus, but by live fire, a well-roofed burning wick called a "match"; and so they could be loaded and discharged time after time in a pouring rain.

There was also a psychological reason. The cannon was professional; if was proof of "legitimacy." It was noisy, heavy, expensive, and it coughed out an enormous blob of smoke. If you had a cannon you meant business. The wild Highlanders who flocked to Bonnie Prince Charlie's banner in '45 called the cannon "the mother of muskets," and it gave them confidence—it made them feel modern, up-to-date—to have one in their midst, no matter how antiquated it might be, or how clumsily manned. The American colonists thought of it in much the same way. Until the outbreak of the Revolution, the cannon, in America, had been only a fortifications piece, not a fieldpiece. It was of course no good against the Indians; but now that the colonists were fighting a war according to the rules, against regulars, it might be very good indeed. The artillery, in the Continental Army, was looked upon as an elite corps.

The boats were not ready, but there was no fuss, no confusion. The men waited patiently, the officers too. Most of the officers around Washington had gloom stamped on their faces, for it seemed certain that the weather was going to win this night, but Washington himself, astride a chestnut sorrel, his favorite, showed no anxiety. Washington indeed, for him, was positively gay. He even twitted Colonel Knox on his waistline; and that made everybody feel better, for the commander-in-chief was not given to jokes, even labored, feeble ones.

Knox himself was ebullient, effervescent—an optimist; but then, he always had been that way. In manner, as in appearance, he was almost the exact opposite of Washington, whose close friend and confidant he had become.

Knox, who had formerly run a book-and-stationery store in Boston, was chief of artillery for the whole army. In addition to his own orders, he relayed those of the commander-in-chief, who seldom had to raise his voice. The head cannoneer had a rich, powerful bass, and it carried well, despite the wind. Many a man was to avow afterward that Henry Knox's voice was one of the things he best remembered about that wild, wild night.

At about eleven o'clock it started to rain, a very cold rain.

The first to cross were the Virginia Continentals under General Adam Stephen. They formed the advance party, and as soon as they reached the New Jersey shore they fanned out into pickets, the object being to keep civilian snoopers away.

These were followed by Mercer's Connecticut, Massachusetts, and Maryland men, most of them Continentals—that is, regular army members. These were crack troops. Then came Stirling with more Virginia Continentals, and Haslet's scrappy Delawareans, and a Pennsylvania rifle regiment. All of these, together with Stephen's vanguard, were to form the first division, under Nathanael Greene.

The rain turned into snow, flakes that hissed as they struck a face.

So far from opposing the landing, or getting in the way, the inhabitants of that rural region of New Jersey turned out in comparatively large numbers to offer their services. They had had a taste of the nearby Hessians, whom they wholeheartedly abhorred.

THE CROSSING OF THE DELAWARE

There was one exception, a farmer from Bucks County, Pennsylvania, who was visiting a friend in that vicinity. Bucks County was known as a hotbed of Toryism, and this man too was a Tory, a convinced one. Soon after the Continentals began to arrive, and it became obvious what their target would be, this man borrowed a horse and rode to Trenton. He was directed to Colonel von Rall's headquarters, the home of the tanner, Stacy Potts, on the west side of King Street, but there he was told that the colonel was dining and playing cards with one Abraham Hunt, a merchant who lived at the corner of King and Second streets; so he went there. This was late, after midnight, but from the sounds the colonel was still at it. A Negro servant came to the door and said that Colonel von Rall was not to be disturbed. The man from Bucks County asked if he could send in a message, and he wrote this, describing what he had seen, and gave it to the Negro, who took it in to Colonel Rall. That personage emitted a contemptuous snort and thrust the paper into his pocket. He did not even try to read it. He didn't bother to have it translated.

The snow-rain ceased shortly before midnight, but that cutting wind still blew out of the northeast.

Washington crossed the river right after Stephen's vanguard, in a boat captained by William Blackler of Marblehead. On the New Jersey shore, his cloak wrapped around him, and his sword tucked between his legs, he sat on a discarded old beehive to supervise the landings. He seldom spoke. He was not a garrulous man.

The watchword for the night, chosen by the commander-in-chief himself, with no notable flash of inspiration, was "Victory or Death."

The second division, Sullivan's, and the cannon, took even longer to get across. They brought Washington his horse, in a later Durham, and he abandoned the beehive.

The original plan had been to assemble in full on the New Jersey bank and start the march south to Trenton—the distance was about nine miles—by midnight. This would allow for a predawn attack and might even leave them time for a bit of breath-catching, so that they could start the fight fresh. It was an old Indian trick to attack just before dawn, when the sleepers' senses are dullest, and was not Washington, after all, an old Indian fighter? From the beginning, however, it was clear that this schedule could not be maintained. It was after three o'clock by the time they were all in order and ready to go. The element of surprise, on which the venture so largely leaned, it would seem had been lost.

Somebody came to Washington with a message from General Sullivan. For all their efforts, many of Sullivan's men had wet powder.

"Then tell the general to use the bayonet," Washington replied, "for I mean to take Trenton tonight."

They marched about a mile to Benjamin Moore's house, and there Washington, still in saddle, had a drink, and there too some of the men ate a little, while others flumped down in the slush to sleep. It was hard getting those sleepers to their feet afterward.

It began to snow again, though it was more like sleet now, very cutting, cruel.

The strictest silence was enjoined. No light was to be shown. Any man who broke out of ranks, they were warned, would be shot.

At Moore's the road split. To the right was the River road, which Sullivan took. To the left was the Pennington road, which Greene's division would take. Washington elected to go with Greene.

These roads were about the same length, and scouts reported that they were in about equally poor condition. The River road, which did in fact more or less follow the winding of the Delaware, would bring Sullivan's men into the lower part of Trenton, near the ferry. The Pennington road would bring Greene's men into the upper or northern part of town, where it was hoped that they could set up their guns at the junction of King and Queen streets, a junction from which the whole town could be controlled or at least terrified by a brisk artillery fire. It was at King and Queen streets that Von Donop had suggested that Rall build a redoubt; but Rall hadn't.

And so, they pushed off.

Chapter

16

Sunrise was to be at seven twenty-three that morning, first light at seven ten, and it was just about this time, a murky time, that the advance guard of Greene's division on the Pennington road came to an abrupt halt, which caused all those behind them to stop likewise, the road was so narrow.

In a field on the left stood a small body of men. Who were they? Farmers? Hessians? What were they doing there? It was still somewhat too early to expect an encounter with the northernmost Hessian outpost, but nobody could be sure.

The Continentals unwrapped their firelocks and cocked them.

The men in the field were hailed, and they answered in English.

By this time General Washington himself, anxious to learn the reason for the pause, had ridden up. He asked who was the leader of these strangers, and a young man stepped forward and identified himself as Richard Anderson, captain, 5th Virginia regiment, Stephen's brigade. And what was he doing here? The brigadier himself had sent them over, the previous day, Christmas, with orders to scout the Hessian outposts to the north and east of Trenton, cautioning them at the same time not to get involved in a fight. In the swirling storm, not long ago, they had stumbled upon a lone German sentinel, whom they shot dead almost before they realized what they were doing. This might result in an alarm, and they thought that they had better return to Pennsylvania, by way of McKonkey's Ferry. They were on their way in that direction now—they hoped. The fact is, they'd been lost.

Brigadier General Stephen was right there to verify this: he was, in fact, the commanding officer of the van. Washington, furious, whirled upon him. Washington never had liked Adam Stephen, a political opponent back in Virginia.

"You, sir, may have ruined all my plans by having put them on their guard!"

He quickly recovered his composure, and in a quiet voice ordered that the stray detatchment take its regular place in Stephen's brigade. The march—or slide, or slog—was resumed.

Christmas was not a day of much celebration in colonial America, any more than it was in Great Britain at that time, but a day for somewhat reserved good cheer, and, as it is in France now, rather a church holiday than an excuse for overeating. In Germany, home of the Christmas tree, the holly wreaths, Kris Kringle, and all the rest, this was not so. To the German, Christmas was a feast, literally.

December 25 had not been picked as the night for an attack on Trenton simply because it *was* Christmas. It had been picked because it was the earliest possible day when supplies could be gathered and other arrangements made. Nevertheless, the leaders hoped that an overcelebration of Christmas Day in the Hessian quarters might help by making the pickets and the members of the outposts drowsy and slow to respond.

If they did so hope, they were to be disappointed. The

Hessians had not let down their guard. So far from guzzling great quantities of *schnapps*, they had scoured the surrounding countryside in vain for anything stronger than some spruce beer, pretty watery stuff for heroes. True, there were forty kegs of rum, but this was not for the troops, even at Christmas: it was for medicinal purposes and the officers. As for wine, the most popular, Madeira, brought three and six a bottle in Trenton, when you could get it at all; and this was far beyond the means of any Hessian soldier. Only officers and sergeants would be likely to have money, anyway. Theoretically, the Hessians were paid in British shillings and pence; but like the British, most of the rank and file were not paid at all until their term of service had run out, the money being withheld on a wide variety of pretexts made possible by an almost unbelievably complicated financial system. This saved the lugging of a huge military chest on the field. It also helped to insure against desertion, for a private with empty pockets is not likely to slip away.

The trudgers on the Pennington road were within two miles of the town when they met the first of the enemy. This was some time between seven thirty and eight o'clock. The snow-rain-sleet drove sullenly and slantingly toward the earth; but it did tend to sop up sounds. Nevertheless, the advance guard under Stephen, closely supported by Mercer's men, distinctly heard the slam-bang of musketry ahead of them, and they heard too the cries of the pickets who ran away: *"Der Feind! Der Feind! Heraus!"* They might not have known what the words meant, but they could make a good guess.[45]

Lieutenant Andreas Wiederhold was just stepping out of his hut, about to make a routine check. He tumbled all the rest of his pickets out, and they fired one shot, and then fled.

They did quite right. They were not there to give battle

but to give instead an alarm. And the Americans were charging through the murk in overwhelming numbers.

The Hessians fell back only a few hundred yards, to the main outpost, a whole company of men of the Rall regiment in command of Captain von Altenbockum. These were already in position, and they too fired just once and then ran, reloading.

At almost the same instant there was a splatter of musketry down near the river, where Sullivan's advance guard had flushed the fifty jägers out of the fine countryhouse of a prominent patriot, Philemon Dickinson, at present sojourning in Philadelphia.

This had been nicely timed. The River road was slightly shorter than the Pennington road, and Sullivan had compensated for this difference by halting his men for a little while halfway.

All the fugitives, jägers and Altenbockum's Ralls, alike, had to run hard to keep away from these fiends from nowhere. It might be expected that after so much slogging through the night the Continentals, wet and weary as they must have been, would attack only with caution. The very opposite was true. It may be that they had been so bored with the march that a little fighting came as a relief. At any rate, they charged, shouting, at top speed.

Von Rall's was the regiment "of the day." That is, it stood all guard duty. Such members as were not posted out of town or at the ferryhouse or the bridge were permitted to sleep in their customary quarters, but they must be in full uniform and have their loaded guns at their sides. This, then, was the first regiment to turn out. It tried to form near the foot of King Street.

At the head of that street, at its northern tip, where it joined Queen Street, the two forming a long thin wedge pointed away from the river, six American cannons had immediately been mounted. Four of these were pointed and promptly started to fire down Queen Street, throwing the emergent Lossbergs into confusion. The other two were hurtling balls down King Street, which did not help the leaderless Ralls. In command of those two guns was young Alexander Hamilton, the diminutive pale dandy with his hat cocked fashionably forward.

Lieutenant Jacob Piel, Rall's brigade adjutant, had to hammer hard at the King Street door before his master appeared, in nightshirt, at an upstairs window. There had been a sneak attack on one of the outposts the previous night by a wandering band of Continentals who fled as soon as they were faced, and it could be that Rall did not take the first scattered firing seriously. Clearly he had made a big time of it the previous night, and he was glassy-eyed. When the cannon began to boom, however, only a few hundred feet away, he snapped to attention. In a few minutes he was out in the street, strapping on his sword, calling for his horse.

Whatever else he might have been, Johann Gottlieb von Rall was no milksop. With a fine disregard for Hamilton's cannonballs or the musketfire from Mercer's men, who had deployed in the field on the Hessian left, he stormed here and there, shouting commands. His own regiment had almost broken, but he rallied it. He ordered the Von Lossbergs into the field between Third and Fourth streets, behind the English church. He ordered the Knyphausen regiment to an orchard on the banks of the Assunpink, where they should form a reserve. Seemingly it was his plan to clear King and Queen streets at the same time with simultaneous bayonet charges. In the midst of his labors he was knocked off his horse by two musket balls in the side, either of which would have been enough to kill him. He was carried into the Methodist church at Queen and Fourth, the unread letter from the Bucks County man still in his pocket. His best epitaph was one given him by his fellow countryman, the historian Von Ochs: "He was a good soldier but a bad general."

Greene's men were spread—Stirling in the center, behind the field guns, ready to receive any charge the Hessians might make up either King or Queen streets, Mercer's men on the right in fields from which they could enfilade the Ralls trying to form in King Street, and Fermoy and Stephen on the left between the Princeton road and Assunpink Creek, a post from which they could contain the badly confused Knyphausens, who were huddled in an orchard. With Sullivan it was different. His men drove on straight ahead, from the River road leading into Front Street—or First Street—and making for the bridge over the creek at the foot of Queen Street. The Americans, it seemed, were everywhere. And they were very busy.

The sealing-off of the Assunpink Creek bridge had been part of the original plan. Ewing wasn't there, as they now learned. Sullivan moved as fast as he could, but there were many Hessians who escaped.

The twenty dragoons of the British 16th all got away. They were supposed to be messengers, not warriors. They never even paused to see whether this was another hit-and-run raid or the real thing. They just saddled up and got out as fast as they could. They looped far around to the left, and later that day brought the news to the British at Princeton.

The jägers got over the bridge—all except one who tripped and was taken prisoner. They had not been trained in battle tactics, and their rifles had no bayonets, so that the best thing they could do was get out of the way. They went straight south, to Bordentown, where they broke the news to Von Donop.

Assorted Hessian grenadiers got over that bridge as well. A body of one hundred men and three officers regularly stationed at the drawbridge over Crosswicks Creek to keep up

The Tide Turns

communications between Trenton and Bordentown easily escaped, since they were four miles south of the Assunpink when the shooting started. Others swam the Assunpink, which a few forded.

The Hessian fieldpieces had not been massed and were not equipped for quick handling. The Ralls did get two brass three-pounders to the foot of King Street, but these were no match for Hamilton's little battery.

Meanwhile, members of Stirling's regiment, individually and in small groups, began to filter down into houses along both of the main streets. They would get inside—very few of the houses were occupied—and dry their locks and flints by rubbing them against their underclothes, or by some other method; and soon they were shooting out of windows in the fashion that Americans liked, the Indian fashion. Until that time there had been plenty of noise, what with the cannons, but very little musketry. The Hessians, most of them, got off only one round, and then their guns were wet.

When a charge was ordered down both of the main streets, the sharpshooters came whooping out of the houses on either side to join it.

One party charged the small Hessian battery at the foot of King Street, and took it, though the officers, two lads still in their teens, were wounded in the process. Captain William Washington, a burly, bashful, slow-smiling fellow, a distant cousin of the commander-in-chief, got both his hands cut, and a slim young man named Monroe, of Wheedon's Virginians, was wounded in the side of the neck.[46]

Major Dechow fell, mortally wounded. The Hessians now were completely surrounded—and completely confused.

There was no *one* surrender. It was piecemeal, all over the place. Somebody did raise a white handkerchief on a stick. The officers, after a dozen hasty consultations, put their hats on the ends of their swords and lifted these high. The men,

SURRENDER OF HESSIAN TROOPS TO GENERAL WASHINGTON AFTER THE BATTLE OF TRENTON

many of them sobbing with rage, slammed their muskets to the ground.

That was the end of the Battle of Trenton. It had taken a little less than two hours, and had been the noisiest, wildest, murkiest, most savage struggle that anybody on either side ever had known—and the most decisive, too.

The Americans had had two privates and two junior officers—Monroe and Washington—slightly wounded; none killed. The Hessians had lost 22 killed and 92 wounded (many of whom died later), 948 prisoners, 6 brass pieces, 6 wagons, 40 horses, 1,000 muskets with bayonets, 15 stands of regimental and company colors, including those taken from the Americans at Fort Washington, 14 drums and all the trumpets, clarionets, and hautboys of two bands, and an incalculable accumulation of loot, mountains of it.

Washington still wasn't satisfied. He wanted to go on fighting.

CHAPTER

17

"25 this day at 12 aClock we march⁴ Down the River about 12 miles. in the Night we Crossed the River Dullerway," Private David How, a mere boy, wrote in his diary. "With a large Body of men and Field Pieces. 26 This morning at 4 aClock We got off with our Field pieces Marched 8 miles to Trenton Whare we are Atacked by a number of Hushing & we Toock 1000 of them besides killed Some Then we march⁴ back And got to the River at Night and got over all the Hushing."[47]

The next day, he laconically records, they washed their shirts.

Not all of the members of the Grand Army took the adventure so casually. In the battle itself, finding energy from God knew where, they had been veritable demons; but when the last shot had been fired, the last prisoner disarmed, some of them were ready to quit, while others started to look around for loot. Had word got out of the commander-in-chief's plan to push on there might well have been trouble. It did not.

The commander-in-chief had suffered from smallpox,

acute pleurisy, influenza, dysentery, something that might have been typhoid,⁴⁸ and something that assuredly was bad teeth; but you would never have guessed this by looking at him. He stood six feet four and a half inches, and he sat ramrod-straight in saddle. He showed granitic. He seemed to be composed not of muscle and bone, nerves and skin tissue, but of steel. *He* would have gone on fighting forever, you might think. But his men were human, and they had taken a great deal.

He was all eagerness to strike while the iron was hot. Here they were on the east bank: Why not take advantage of this? What about hitting Von Donop at Bordentown? or Leslie at Princeton? or even Grant at New Brunswick, where a swift stroke might at the same time free General Lee, who was still a prisoner there? It seemed possible. Anything, in that first flush of victory, seemed possible.

His aides and advisors shook their heads, and they pointed to the scene about them.

The storm had not abated. If anything, it had grown worse. The boats were not here at Trenton, but nine miles upriver, and to get back to them would mean to march almost directly into that terrible northeast wind.

Not only were many of the men on the verge of collapse, but more than a few were drunk. They had discovered those forty kegs of rum, and until officers came upon them and stove the kegs in they had made more or less merry. Such cases could he forced to march back to the ferry, if they were told that they would be left behind otherwise, but they could not be made to fight again—not, at least, for some time.

And there were the prisoners to be thought of, and the guns, and the horses.

Also, how would the men be fed? Whether because many had not obeyed the order to take three days' rations, or whether because in accordance with a common practice of the day they had shucked off their knapsacks just before going into action and now could not find them again, the men were hungry. Very little food had been found in the Hessians' storehouse; and in this weather foragers obviously would not bring in much.

So Washington sighed, and acquiesced.

That return trip was hell. They had taken the paroles of the Hessian sick and wounded, whom they could not carry, for they were sick themselves, they were wounded with weariness, so that they could hardly walk. Conditions on the river were at least as bad, perhaps worse, and the job took much longer because of the added equipment and supplies, not to mention the prisoners, who, however, turned out to be a good-natured lot, if still stunned.[49] It took all afternoon and most of the night to get back to the other bank, and some of the units were not released to their tents until almost dawn. About a third of them, next morning, reported themselves on sick list.

John Cadwalader was an energetic and resourceful officer, and a natural leader of men, but he had not had much experience in the field and he had never before held high command. He knew that the great Horatio Gates had once been thought of for this southern river command, and like most amateurs he was humble in the presence of a real practitioner of war. When he heard that not only his own Philadelphia Associators but also the New England Continentals under his command were complaining that he had failed them by keeping them up all night in that biting rain-snow, and then backing away from the Jersey shore after all, he was hurt. And when next morning he heard the sound of cannonading across the river, up near Trenton, he could hardly believe his ears. He sent a message to General Ewing of the Pennsylvania militia, who was stationed just opposite Trenton and could see the other side through a spyglass; and Ewing replied that there had indeed been a battle over there, and that it looked as though Washington had won.

Red of face, Cadwalader sprang into action. He had failed his commander! After Herculean labors, in daylight this time, he got his entire force of militiamen and New Englanders, besides a large number of fieldpieces, across the river to a point near Burlington.

Everything was strangely quiet. Where were the Hessians? Burlington was a ghost town. Colonel Reed, who had been out on a scouting mission—a Philadelphian now, he knew this territory well, for he had been born in Trenton and had gone to college at Princeton—assured Cadwalader that Bordentown, which is where Von Donop was supposed to be, was utterly motionless. Cadwalader wavered; but at last he crept up on Bordentown.

It, too, turned out to have been deserted. The only persons they found there were some Hessian sick in a small and very dirty hospital. There was not even any livestock, and there was every evidence that the departure had been hurried, things snatched right and left.

The same applied to Crosswicks Creek, an important post, where not so much as a ripped-off uniform button was found, though there was ample proof that the place had lately been occupied.

This is what had happened: The Hessians who fled from the scene of hostilities, bug-eyed and splattered with mud, had not wished to have it known that they had run away from just any old army, and so they had cried out about the great masses of rebels who swept irresistibly down upon them; the smallest estimate was 6,000.

The same thing happened with the 30-odd Hessians and the 20 British dragoons who had made it to Princeton. Their stories were even taller; so that by the time the news got to New York, the following day, the figure generally believed was 20,000. Why not? How could a lesser force expect to take over such sterling regiments as the Ralls, the Lossbergs, the Knyphausens? The fact was, of course, that Washington had had only about 2,400 men.

Von Donop was no fool. His had been the last link in the chain, and the fall of Trenton meant that he would be cut off from his base and at the mercy of that enormous horde of rebels unless he acted with speed. He did have to leave his sick behind, yes; but at least his men got most of their loot away.

Cadwalader, holding his breath, pushed on to Trenton itself. Here he found the Hessian sick and wounded, especially the wounded, and half a handful or less of still-frightened townspeople, and here too he learned that Washington had gone back to Pennsylvania.

Now he *was* in a box! He was alone in New Jersey, as you might say. Neither the British nor the Hessians could be expected to take a thing like Trenton lying down. They would soon be back, in vast numbers, looking for blood.

Cadwalader did not panic; but he did waver for a while. He thought of returning to Bristol, Pennsylvania, while there was still time to return. But he was dissuaded from this. Morale, morale. "These men have crossed three times in the past twenty-four hours," an officer told him, "and they don't want to even *see* the damn' river again for a while." Cadwalader reluctantly agreed.

He needed a leader. He would have written to Washington, suggesting that Washington recross the Delaware and together with his own troops and the 1,600 new Pennsylvania militiamen just landed at Bordentown, slash the enemy again before they had fully recovered; only he learned that Colonel Reed already had done so.

There was nothing that Washington would have liked better. So few days were left! But again, he had to think of his troops. Through another of those commissariat snarls that always seemed to happen at the wrong time, there was a shortage of fresh food, so that the veterans of Trenton were not only weary but hungry as well. They would need a little more time to get back their strength.

Not until December 29 did Washington again venture forth, and then he encountered the worst crossing yet. It took all that afternoon, all night, and a good part of the daylight hours of the next morning. When at last he stood on the east bank with his 1,500 men around him—all who were still ablebodied—he learned with dismay that the British already were on the march. Howe would have taken a week to think it over before he moved; but it was not like that with Cornwallis, who hastily ordered all his luggage off that ship destined for England, and took to the road, summoning to his side Leslie, Von Donop, and Grant. They were right at this moment converging or about to converge upon Princeton, only a few miles from where Washington stood.

Cornwallis, reports had it, commanded at least 8,000 men, the cream of the British Army. Washington had a bare 5,000 and his back was to the river.

He marched to Trenton, and called Cadwalader in from Crosswicks Creek, the militiamen up from Bordentown. He started to dig in on the south side of Assunpink Creek, facing the town.

This must have looked like madness. Washington had no sure line of retreat, no nearby woods or hills to take to, no massed boats, his right was protected by the river, but his left was up in the air. He did have a small superiority in guns, but they were not very good guns and not well handled, and they would be of use only in the event of a direct frontal attack, which was unlikely. Why should the British storm the sixteen-foot-wide bridge over the Assunpink or try one of the close-in fords that Washington would surely have posted? All they needed to do was hook around to the left, to a point where the creek could be waded, and strike at Washington's unfortified right. The ground there was all bare and flat, the sort of country in which the British regulars were at their best and the Continentals at their worst. From there, Washington and all his men could be pushed back against the river and systematically slaughtered.

Yet Washington knew what he was doing.

First, he had to take steps to hold his army together. The newly raised Pennsylvania militiamen could be expected to stay around for a while, but they were absolutely raw, without even parade-ground experience. The regulars were ready to quit. The attitude of the average Continental was: I've done my part, now let somebody else do his.

Those Pennsylvania militiamen had been enlisted, in a miraculously short time, by the efforts of General Thomas Mifflin, who had a silver tongue. Washington had brought Mifflin over with him this time, and he and Henry Knox, with his roly-poly belly and his deep bass voice—and he was only twenty-six!—addressed them by regiments. Washington himself addressed them. He hated public speaking, but it was all a part of his job.

He offered each soldier a ten-dollar bonus, besides the regular pay, if he would re-enlist for a six-week term; and he pledged his personal, private fortune that this would be paid, no matter what Congress might or might not do. He also promised them that they would have their share of any loot that might be recovered from the British or the Hessians, and that they could keep, trade, or sell this loot, as they pleased.

Whether swayed by the oratory or moved by their commanding officer's noble offer, after a little hesitation most of the men did consent to re-enlist, raising their muskets to signify this. An exception was—of all outfits!—John Glover's Marbleheaders. A few of these consented to stay, and a few more agreed to enlist in the Delaware River "navy" of Com-

HENRY KNOX, CHIEF OF ARTILLERY, CONTINENTAL ARMY

modore Thomas Seymour, but most of them had been stricken by the privateering fever that raged along the Atlantic coast at that time. They wanted to get aboard of a vessel—any vessel, so long as she carried a letter of marque—and make some real money. What was a ten-dollar bonus to a privateer?

New Year's Day of 1777 the last of Cornwallis's troops joined him at Princeton, as spies unquestionably informed Washington, who thereupon sent out a delaying party under Chevalier Matthias Alexis Roche de Fermoy, one of the first of the European military adventurers who were about to inundate the Continental Army. De Fermoy had a fondness for the bottle, and when he pleaded indisposition and went back to the banks of the Assunpink it was generally whispered that he was drunk. No matter. The command then fell to the second ranking officer, and he was perfect for it—Colonel Edward Hand, a gangling, drawling, skinny man, bald as an egg, sharp as a crab apple, whose Pennsylvania rifles were just about the best in the business. Hand also had under him that day Colonel Hausegger's Pennsylvania German battalion, Colonel Charles Scott's Virginia Continental regiment, and two guns of Captain Thomas Forrest's battery. They posted themselves that night, Wednesday night, at Five Mile Run, and the enemy appeared early the next morning.

The enemy appeared early, but not bright. It was a disagreeable, overcast day. The cold spell had been broken, but the air still was chilly. It had rained hard the previous night, and the road, such as it was, was calf-deep in mud.

This was to be a long day, dawn to sunset. The British advanced at an average of one mile an hour. Time after time they came to a full stop—while flushing parties were sent ahead to root out the pesky rebels, who thereupon faded away. The Americans made use of every rock and tree, every fence and fold. Their orders were to delay the enemy until dark, and this they did superbly well.

The vanguard of the enemy army was largely made up of jägers. There were to be sundry direct clashes, during this war, between the jägers on one side and the Pennsylvania long riflemen on the other, but this one, this Princeton-to-Trenton delaying action, is generally considered the best. The jägers would reload a bit faster, because their guns had short barrels, but the Pennsylvanians shot straighter.

Casualties were not great, but it had been a long, grueling march, and even when they got to Trenton, just after sunset, the British were fired upon from many windows before they could mass to rush the Assunpink bridge.

They rushed that bridge several times, but they did not take it. Once they had brought up their artillery and their real shock troops they would probably be able to take it; but the men were tired, and a direct attack would be much more costly than a flank encirclement in the morning. Sir William Erskine, one of his most valued aides, urged the British commander to go at it and finish the job there and then, but Cornwallis shook his head.

"Tomorrow will be time enough to bag the fox," he said.

Next morning, however, the fox wasn't there. Neither were any of his men, or any of his guns. A skimpy working squad, about four hundred, just enough to keep the campfires burning and maintain the sounds of digging, was hurrying off to the east; and that was that.

Where had all the others gone?

This was answered for Cornwallis when he heard the sound of cannonading from the direction of Princeton.

His rear guard!

CHAPTER

18

A SNEAK NIGHT MARCH, to be successful, calls for a great deal of careful staff work and also a great deal of luck. Unexpected, unpredictable obstacles can throw the timetable out of kilter. It was so before Trenton, and it was to be so before Princeton. Nevertheless, this was a very brilliant bit of generalship.

The weather cooperated. It turned suddenly cold, and the mud was frozen underfoot. This made it possible to take most of the cannons, without which no proper army would consider itself complete. The Continentals had almost forty of these—rather poor iron pieces for the most part, but essential for the esteem of the soldiers. The chief of artillery, Knox, did not use his booming bass this night on the south bank of the Assunpink. Indeed, all the preliminaries and all the changes in the first part of the march were conducted in whispers. The wheels of the biggest guns and of those nearest to the creek were swathed in cloths, to soften the sound. Some officers even loosened their sword belts lest these creak.

Nobody under the rank of brigadier knew where they were going or why.

Some talk was to be heard afterward of a mysterious "secret" route. There was no such thing. The road the Continentals took to the hamlet of Sandtown was a new one, but this did not mean that it was hidden or "secret." In part it was cluttered with tree stumps, which in the darkness—and it was a very dark night—often tripped the men and hindered the passage of the guns. Cornwallis must have known of that road, unless his intelligence was asleep. It probably never even occurred to him that an army that had fought so hard and marched so far as the one he faced across the creek would dream of making such a difficult trip. The Continentals did have a couple of local guides, to be sure, but they could have done without them. Colonel Reed alone, to name only one, must have known every foot of the way.

Because of various unforseen delays the start was late—almost one o'clock. The distance was about twelve miles, wide around the British left flank in Trenton, well to the east of the village of Maidenhead,[50] roughly halfway between Trenton and Princeton, where it was probable that Cornwallis would have left part of his rear guard, and so to the goal—Princeton itself, the seat of the now deserted College of New Jersey. The plan was to get there before dawn and to attack right away, but it was broad daylight by the time they even came into sight of the town.

Cornwallis had indeed left a detachment at Maidenhead —General Leslie and the 2nd Brigade, upward of 1,000 men; and at Princeton itself he had left the 4th Brigade, which consisted of the 17th, 40th, and 55th regiments—1,200 men in all—under Lieutenant Colonel Charles Mawhood. Both of these officers had orders to start for Trenton first thing in the morning, and Mawhood at least was already on his way, leading the 17th and part of the 55th, with the rest of the 55th not far behind, while the 40th stayed in town to guard the supplies.

Mawhood had in addition three troops of light dragoons, and one of these was with him. He himself bestrode a small brown horse, and a couple of pet spaniels frisked around him. He might have been John Peel.

It was intensely cold, a morning of bright silver frost that coated everything—one grand glitter.

General Mercer, the Scottish physician, and his brigade, had been told off to the left, to destroy a small bridge over Stony Brook, and so help to cut off those at Princeton from those at Maidenhead and at Trenton. He sallied out of the woods, making in that direction, with Cadwalader's Associators just behind him. He spotted Mawhood at just about the time that Mawhood spotted him, and they flew at one another like a couple of gamecocks.

It never occurred to Mawhood that he was face to face with a part of the main American Army. He assumed as a matter of course that Milord Cornwallis had trounced the rebels at Trenton, and that this group of tousled men was a lost segment of what was left.

The two forces were about equal in number. Each went for a high orchard, a good place from which to fight. The Americans got there first because they had been nearer. They fired three rounds at the redcoats, who responded with only one, much too high, and then came in with fixed bayonets.

This, as it had been so many times before, was too much for the Americans, few of whom had bayonets. They turned tail and ran.

Mawhood chased them to another, nearby rise, and from there he saw, to his dumbfoundment, a second group of men emerging from that same wood. Here were the Associators.

Mercer's horse, a gray, had been shot under him, its leg broken, and he was on his feet with his sword in his fist trying to rally his men when the British came upon him. They knocked him down with their musket butts. They bayonetted him at least seven times. He feigned death, and they went away.

John Haslet was a colonel without a regiment. On the night of Trenton he had fallen from one of the boats into the icy Delaware, and as a result his legs were badly swollen. But he wouldn't quit. His Delaware regiment, or what was left of it, decided to go home; but the colonel stayed on. Now, on foot, and no doubt suffering, but game, he tried to rally Mercer's men. A bullet caught him in the head, killing him instantly.

The British were in a murderous mood that morning. Poor young Lieutenant Bartholomew Yeates, whose ankle had been broken, dragged himself under a wagon in a nearby farmyard, and the redcoats when they sought him out there not only shot and clubbed him but also bayonetted him thirteen times, though all the while he was begging for quarter.

Captain John Fleming of the 1st Virginia and Captain Neil of the New Jersey artillery also were shot dead while fighting.

All this had taken only a few minutes.

When Mawhood saw that he was meeting a larger force than he had expected, he withdrew his men to a low place between the orchard and the second rise of ground, where he deployed them behind a fence. The Philadelphia Associators came up, and Cadwalader led them to a spot within fifty yards of the fence, where he tried to get them to file off and fire in platoons. This was too much. They had done it on the parade ground, but never with bullets flying around them and within sight of those dreaded bayonets. They too broke and ran. Cadwalader was having some success in rallying them when a new actor burst upon the scene.

George Washington had heard the firing on his left, and he dashed in that direction. He rode to a point not more than fifty-five or sixty feet from the fence before he reined to a halt, all the while waving his hat and shouting encouragement to those behind him. One of his aides, an impressionable young Irishman named Fitzgerald, drew *his* hat down over his eyes, for he could not bear to see his beloved general killed. There was a volley, and Fitzgerald flashed a look. He had forgotten that English soldiers were the worst shots in the world. The smoke floated away and there was Washington, still waving his hat, still shouting encouragement.

Washington was trying to tell them that all they had to do was charge and the day was theirs. This was true, and Mawhood knew it was true—now. Though it must have pained him, Mawhood ordered a retreat. You can't fight a whole army.

The British behaved well for a little while, despite the odds, but once they had reached the Princeton-Trenton road, and even though a troop of dragoons tried to cover their retreat, they broke and ran. Some stayed on the road; others took to the open fields and to the woods. The Continentals pelted down the road after them, Washington at their head, still waving his hat and whooping for joy. Who then was the fox, and who the hunter?

The redcoats had shrugged off their knapsacks just before going into action, and these were all left behind. Now they threw away their muskets as they ran. Some escaped into the woods, others were killed, and about 50 were taken prisoner.

Meanwhile, the rear division of the 55th had retreated into the town, where it joined the 40th. Attacked, some of these men broke away for New Brunswick. Others for a short time defended a redoubt. Many took refuge in the college building, Nassau Hall. A single cannon shot dislodged these last, who came out one by one to cast their muskets on the ground. There were 194 of them. Some 20 American prisoners were released from Nassau Hall at the same time.

The whole business had taken only three-quarters of an hour. Continental casualties had been about 40, including some of the best officers in the army. The British casualties numbered about 400, most of them prisoners.

Two brass six-pounders had been seized, but the Americans had to leave these behind: no horses. There were seven wagonloads of assorted loot, a lot of gunpowder and other military supplies, and, blessedly, many blankets. There was also a great deal of forage, but they could only burn this.

Many of the wounded were in horrible shape, the fighting had been at such close quarters. The Continental surgeons did whatever they could for these. There was no time to bury the dead. Cornwallis would soon be back. Two hours after the end of hostilities the Continentals were marching out at one end of Princeton while the British advance guard was entering the other end.

The Continentals went northeast, the direction of New Brunswick. This was just what Cornwallis had feared. The town on the Raritan was only lightly garrisoned, for he had drawn troops from it for his own present force. In addition, it contained huge stores, and its military chest lately had been increased to the tune of £70,000, gold. Washington did not know about the military chest, but Cornwallis did. Seventy thousand pounds sterling would have done wonders to the tottering Continental credit.

Washington called a conference of general officers right on the road, on their horses, somewhere near Rocky Hill. Should they risk it? They decided that they should not, which must have broken the commander-in-chief's heart. It would be asking too much of the men, some of whom had not been allowed to sleep, even standing up, for more than forty hours.

If he could only have had 600 or 700 *fresh* soldiers, Washington was to tell Congress in his report, he would have taken the chance. But there was nobody fresh in that bedraggled army. So they turned north for Somerville and Morristown, a center of patriotic fervor, where they built themselves huts and holed up; and then the campaign really *was* over.

Chapter 19

THE WAR should have been over, but it was not. In Great Britain, where the ministers of state had been fed rosy bulletins about Howe's consummate generalship, the news of Trenton—the British never did admit that Princeton had been a real battle, much less a defeat for them—burst like a bombshell. It had been confidently supposed, until then, that the next report from America would be to the effect that the rebels had unconditionally laid down their arms. Shares had gone up in anticipation of this. Fetes had been planned.

In New York, the nearer place, officers and officials had been more realistic, but even they had not supposed that there would be any further campaigning until spring. Even wellwishers believed that the American cause, already so weakened that it could scarcely stand, would not survive the winter. It would collapse; and then at last men could go home, where so many of them so heartily wished to be.

But now it appeared that the corpse had come to life and was fighting with both fists.

Trenton-Princeton made George Washington a world figure. In all the chancelleries of Europe they talked about

The Tide Turns

him, this quiet man. Until now, except among the British in the field, who had a healthy respect for his abilities, he had shown as a somewhat vague, and certainly minor, personage, and to some he had even smacked of charlatanry—maybe a Corsican brigand, colorful, unpredictable, in general to be applauded, but not ever to be taken seriously. It was different after Trenton. France, for one, became much more interested, so that an alliance loomed. The Continental credit, which had been plunging, stiffened—at least briefly.

The victories did not lessen desertion and quitting in the Continental Army. The boys still determinedly left camp as soon as their terms of enlistment ended—if they did not go sooner—whole companies and even regiments at a time. Trenton-Princeton, however, did sharply stimulate enlistments. All through the colonies there was a surge of enthusiasm for the patriot cause, and men who had previously been undecided suddenly made up their minds to do a part.

Even Nicholas Cresswell, an Englishman recently arrived in America, a civilian, and as pronounced a Tory as it would have been possible to find, conceded this. He wrote:

> Monday, Jan 6th, 1777. News that Washington had taken 760 Hessian prisoners at Trenton in the Jerseys. Hope it is a lie. This afternoon hear he had likewise taken six pieces of Brass Cannon. Tuesday, Jan. 7th, 1777. The News is confirmed. The minds of the people are much altered. A few days ago they had given up the cause for lost. Their late successes have turned the scale and now they are all liberty mad again. Their Recruiting parties could not get a man (except he brought him from his master) no longer since last week, and now the men are coming in by companies . . . This has given them new spirits, got them fresh succours and will prolong the War, perhaps for two years. They have recovered

their panic and it will not be an easy matter to throw them into that confusion again.

Cresswell underestimated. The war in fact was to last five more years, and they were to be agonizing years. More than once it was to look as though the Continental cause would be snuffed out, as the Continental credit sank and sank. Yet never again were the spirits of the patriots to be so low. They had passed their darkest hour, and they were stumbling toward the light.

"Tell the Colonel he is safe," retorted cocky General Grant, in charge of all New Jersey after Cornwallis had started to make plans to return to England. The colonel he referred to was Rall, who had asked for more troops to keep up his communications with Princeton and New Brunswick. "I will undertake to keep the peace in New Jersey with a corporal's guard," Grant had added.

He sang a different song now. That Trenton and Bordentown, Princeton too, should be evacuated, was only common sense, what with Washington and his reported 12,000 to 15,000 men—Von Donop's official estimate—cutting a swathe right up the middle of the state. The British went even further. They pulled out of Newark and Elizabethtown as well, and out of Hackensack. A few days earlier they had, properly, considered New Jersey their own. Now the only footholds they kept in that state were Paulus Hook,[51] an outpost that had to be supplied by sea, and the lower Raritan Valley—the Amboys and Brunswick.

The men crowded into the Raritan Valley, though they did have shoes and blankets, were almost as uncomfortable as those Washington commanded at Morristown. Washington did not have the men or the money or the supplies to leave his strong position and attack in force, but he did harass the enemy with small parties. He was unrelenting about this.

The Tide Turns 149

Anything any of the Raritan redcoats got from the surrounding countryside they had to fight for. Practically all of their food, fuel, and fodder came from New York City, most of it by way of Staten Island. There was much grumbling.

The war, in truth, had assumed the form that it was to hold to the end. The British and Hessians, though they remained overwhelmingly superior in strength, were on the defensive. They were looked upon as invaders now, and were hated as such. Their authority extended just as far as their guns would shoot, and not a step farther.

The sufferings of the Raritan garrison were of little concern to those Britishers lucky enough, or influential enough, to have themselves stationed in New York City. *They* had something more exciting to think about. General Howe was to become a knight.

His formal notification had said that this was because of his "unintermitted ambition to serve your King and country" —i.e., because he had won the Battle of Long Island; but one disgruntled loyalist, crusty old Judge Jones, wrote that it was rather "a reward for *evacuating* Boston, for *lying indolent* upon Staten Island for near two months, for *suffering* the whole rebel army to escape him upon Long Island, and again at White Plains; for *not putting an end to rebellion* in 1776, when so often in his power; for making such *injudicious cantonments* of his troops in Jersey as he did, and for *suffering* 10,000 veterans under experienced generals, to be cooped up in Brunswick, and Amboy, for nearly six months, by about 6,000 militia, under the command of an inexperienced general."[52]

Whatever the reason, he was to be invested with all the glittering, shimmering insignia of the Most Honorable Order of the Bath and dubbed a Knights Companion thereof. Unlike Cornwallis, unlike Clinton, he could not afford a vacation, and so the ceremony, a splendid one, would be held in New York.

The Order of the Bath might have been honorable but it was by no means ancient: it had been founded by George I a scant half-century ago. Yet it was, assuredly, exclusive. It was made up of the Sovereign himself; a Grand Master, presently Viscount Weymouth; and thirty-six Knights Companions.[53] A member had only the title "sir," his wife only that of "lady," but they preceded mere Knights Bachelors and *their* ladies, and on state occasions they wore a scarlet mantle, a scarlet ribband with the badge of the order pendant therefrom, in gold, as well as a golden collar with golden crowns linked with knots enameled white, and engraved with the motto of the order: *Tria Iuncta in Uno*. So this award was not to be sneered at.

To Admiral Lord Howe were sent the mantle and pendant and other insignia, and he was authorized to act for his sovereign in the dubbing of his brother and for the Grand Master and various other nonpresent members in the ceremonial bathing, the all-night vigil, the putting-to-bed—but not with Mrs. Loring this time—and all the rest of the pseudomedieval claptrap.

Ordinarily the Christmas holidays would have been seized upon as ideal for this investiture and for the public spree that would perforce follow, but what Germain was to call in a letter the "disagreeable occurrence" at Trenton, December 26, made this inadvisable, and the date was moved to the Queen's birthday instead.[54]

It was a gala occasion. The officers wore their dress uniforms and their brightest swords. The sailors were released from their ships, the soldiers from their barracks, and there was music and dancing in the streets. There was a huge banquet. There were fireworks off the southern tip of the island. A great deal of champagne was consumed.

The Tide Turns

The men at Morristown had no champagne. They had frozen toes. They had smallpox, which swept like a wave across the town and camp alike. They had parade duty and guard duty in the worst winter any of them could remember. They had hardtack and water. But they also had faith in their cause; and they were to prevail.

NOTES

1. *Journal*, pp. 82–83. Proceedings of the Massachusetts Historical Society, 1858–1860, first series, IV.
2. "I have heard the bullets whistle, and, believe me, there is something charming in the sound," he had written to his brother John after his first brush on the frontier, just before the formal outbreak of the French and Indian War. *Writings*, I, 70.
3. *Writings*, IV, 451.
4. The naming of battles is a haphazard business. The Germans call Blenheim Höchstädt. The French call Crécy Wadicourt. Waterloo was not fought at Waterloo but three to five miles away, between Mont-Saint-Jean and Plancenoit: it got the name because it was from the village of Waterloo that Wellington wrote the dispatch announcing his victory. The Germans call it La Belle Alliance because that was the farm where Wellington and Blücher met, hours after the fighting—none of which took place there—had ended. And so it goes. There is no reason why historians should wax indignant—as so many have—because the Battle of Bunker Hill

was not recorded as the Battle of Breed's Hill, which is where most of the action took place. Breed's Hill was an outpost, though a vital one, nearer to Boston, nearer to the shore, and not as high as Bunker, or Bunker's, Hill, the object of the fighting. Once Breed's Hill fell, Bunker, not yet fully fortified, was sure to follow. Both names were local, and not at that time official. General Gage in his report, and a contemporary historian, Stedman, refer to the Battle of Bunker's Hill. In letters of the time it was called, usually, the Battle of Charlestown. Of course the most accurate name (if it didn't happen to be too late for accuracy) would be the Battle *for* Bunker Hill. That's what it really was.

5. A regiment then was not like a regiment today. For one thing, it was not nearly as big. In the British Army at that time there was a top number of 477 officers and men—that is, when the regiment was at full strength, which it very seldom was. Six of these and sometimes more would be "warrant men," fictitious soldiers carried on the lists for the purpose of using their pay—which was *not* fictitious—to form a fund for war widows and the like. Besides, the sick list, even in times of peace, might at any given time be as high as 25 percent. A cavalry regiment was just about half the size, in manpower. Curtis, *British Army in the American Revolution*, Appendix 1.

6. "It is difficult to believe that these vessels were not specially re-christened for the voyage, and that Admiral Lord Howe had nothing to do with it." Trevelyan, II, 261 n.

7. Now called the Jumel Mansion, the house is still standing in what today is Roger Morris Park, between One hundred sixtieth and One hundred sixty-second streets.

8. The line was crossed only occasionally by alert, self-educated men, but even these had to pose as noblemen in accordance with the convention. Thus, the two most influential Europeans to join the American Continental Army

(after the Marquis de Lafayette) were Baron de Kalb and Baron von Steuben. Neither was in fact a baron, and Kalb wasn't entitled to that "de" any more than Steuben was entitled to a "von." But they were good soldiers.

9. Yet the hunting shirt was seen on Breed's Hill. A crack militia company from Wethersfield, Connecticut, had its own uniform, a bright and fancy one, but before going into Charlestown peninsula as reinforcements its members were careful to pull hunting shirts over these uniforms, the only ones on the American side. They did this despite the fact that it was a scorching hot day. They did not want to be singled out as officers.

10. Adams (for the word is his: *Works*, IX, 443–44) did not by this mean *sedan* chairs. These still were popular in the large cities of Europe, but they had never gained a foothold in America, in part because of a lack of laborers or lackeys who would serve as chairmen. Franklin did own one, a gift from a friend in Europe, and it was helpful on days when his gout bothered him; but his chairmen, used only intermittently, were trusties borrowed from the state prison, and as such they would not be allowed to go out of Pennsylvania. The vehicle Adams undoubtedly meant was the American "chair," or, as it was usually pronounced in his own New England, "cheer." This was also called a "shay," from the French *chaise*, or chair. It was a fast, two-wheeled, low-slung gig, something like a ricksha pulled by a horse. Oliver Wendell Holmes has immortalized it.

11. In a letter to "dear Abby." *Works*, IX, 443–44.

12. The present Ward's and Randall's islands, respectively.

13. The bay has since been filled in. It was at the foot of East Thirty-fourth Street.

14. The place where they parted company is the present Madison Square. The Bloomingdale road was approx-

imately the modern Broadway, the Post road approximately the modern Lexington Avenue, though neither was notably straight and there were local variations. A narrow country lane connected them exactly at what is now Forty-second Street.

15. That cornfield is now the Grand Central Terminal.

16. This eminence later was renamed Murray Hill, after the owner. Were the house there today it would be straddling Park Avenue between Thirty-sixth and Thirty-seventh streets.

17. Respectively, now, Princeton and Columbia.

18. The space between them was roughly the present-day Central Park. It was thickly wooded then, and much wilder—though it was also safer—than it is now.

19. The late Robert E. Sherwood even wrote a play about it, *Small War on Murray Hill*. Mrs. Murray is not the first female to have such a story told about her. The Countess of Kilmarnock, for example, is supposed to have breakfasted General Hawley so lavishly at Callander House that for a long time she kept him from Falkirk Moor, where a battle was joined, and thus gave Bonnie Prince Charlie and his wild Highlanders a chance to sweep the field. And there must be many others. The character is irresistible.

20. The most forward of these, the southernmost, was on a line with today's One hundred and forty-seventh Street.

21. This action took place approximately over what is now the campus of Columbia University.

22. Third Avenue and Sixty-fifth Street now.

23. ". . . for in this matter, as in all others, those who wish to hear what George Washington has to say in his own defense must wait until the day of Judgement." Trevelyan, II, 276–77.

24. The present Pelham Bay Park.

25. Billias, p.5.

26. They were not cavalry, really, but dragoons, which were mounted infantry. On this occasion, though, they fought on horseback; and the Continentals were in no position to split hairs.

27. Many a time she kept the General in bed when he should have been up and doing, so that it came to be said that the success of American arms was due in large part to the success of hers. But that was later. At the time of the initial occupation of New York, American arms had *had* no success. Blumenthal, *Camp Followers*, 34–36.

The following year the General, who meanwhile had been knighted in recognition of his valor on Long Island, took the lady with him to Philadelphia, where many others besides Quakers stood aghast. This gave rise to sundry verses, some of them anonymous, like:

> *Awake, arouse, Sir Billy.*
> *There's forage in the plain.*
> *Ah! leave your little Filly,*
> *And open the campaign.*
> *Heed not a woman's prattle,*
> *Which tickles in the ear,*
> *But give the word for battle,*
> *And grasp the warlike spear.*

Others, like the verse in Francis Hopkinson's "The Battle of the Kegs," despite the coy use of dashes, were more outspoken:

> *Sir William, he, snug as a flea,*
> *Lay all this while a-snoring;*
> *Nor dream'd of harm as he lay warm*
> *In bed with— —*

They say that even Washington smiled when he heard that one. Moore, *Songs and Ballads*. Tyler, *Literary History*.

28. Now Washington Heights.

29. When Belcher (see BIBLIOGRAPHY) came forth with his *The First American Civil War*, fifty-odd years ago, many were puzzled. Had there been more than one? they asked.

30. East Jersey and West Jersey became legally one in 1702, but the popular differentiation, and the term "the Jerseys," persisted for many years. The line was first drawn from Little Egg Harbor on the Atlantic to a point on the Delaware River at forty-one degrees forty minutes north latitude, thus giving East Jersey about three-eighths, West Jersey about five-eighths, of the province.

31. Now the city of Passaic.

32. "For any effect which they produced upon the general result of the war, they might have been as usefully, and much more agreeably, billeted in the town of the same name in the Isle of Wight." Trevelyan, II, 20.

33. Lee was born January 26, 1732; Washington on February 11, 1732. These dates are in the Old Style, or Julian Calendar, generally in use in North America and Great Britain then. The New Style, or Gregorian Calendar, would have the dates February 6 and February 22, the day we now celebrate as Washington's birthday. The difference of sixteen days remains.

34. *Writings*, VI, 398.

35. One of these was a lieutenant named Banastre Tarleton, who was later to become notorious for his cruelties in the Carolinas, where he served as a lieutenant colonel of horse. His name is still execrated in those parts, but whatever else might be said of him he cannot be denied that often overworked adjective "dashing."

36. Washington never heard of it. Nobody did, until

seventy years after Lee's death. On the face of it, it would seem to convict Lee of treason, but there are reasons to think that the man truly was trying to end the war to the advantage of the colonies, reasons ably set forth by John Richard Alden, the General's latest biographer (see BIBLIOGRAPHY). Professor Alden's personal stand is shown by the subtitle of his book: "Patriot or Traitor?"

37. Now Broad and Warren streets, respectively.

38. "Let them come! We want no trenches! We'll go at them with the bayonet!"

39. Now Columbus, New Jersey.

40. This was done as well with John Honeyman, who, despite the risks of his calling, was to live to be ninety-three. Trevelyan, III, 93–94.

41. In fairness to Gates, it should be said that there is no documentary evidence that any such plot existed. However, there was a great deal of talk—talk which was to increase a few months later when Gates accepted the surrender of Burgoyne at Saratoga. Gates was not as eccentric and not as self-centered a man as Charles Lee, but he probably had as poor an opinion of Washington's military ability and probably itched to take over. Like Lee he had served with distinction in the British Army, though he had not risen as high: he was a major.

42. There were then no bridges over the Delaware. Just to make the whole thing more confusing, on the New Jersey shore McKonkey's Ferry was always called Johnson's Ferry.

43. Wilkinson, *Memoirs*, I, 127–28. Wilkinson was a monumental liar, but there is no reason to believe that he spun this particular yarn out of his imagination. He would have no reason to.

44. Most Americans unfortunately get their idea of Washington's famous "crossing"—actually he crossed the

Delaware six times in the course of this 1776 campaign alone—from the heroic if idiotic picture by Emanuel Leutze, a resident of Wittenberg, Germany, who came over to this country in 1851 to do the work. The original, which measures 21 by 12 feet, is in the basement of the Metropolitan Museum of Art, New York City, and is likely to remain there for a long while, but copies hang in just about every schoolhouse in the land. This is too bad. That puny craft Leutze depicted would look like a mere slab-sided catamaran alongside of a real Durham boat. Even a small Durham was five or six times as big. Leutze evidently had his native Rhine in mind when he sketched the background shoreline, which does not look anything like the Delaware above Trenton. There is no wind. Everything is blessedly dry, though in fact it was pouring. John Glover assuredly would have winced could he see his boys mishandling any boat the way those lubbers are shown doing, and George Washington surely had too much sense to stand with one foot on the thwarts when at any moment he might be pitched into the river. Funniest is the flag. Why it should be displayed at all on a rainy-snowy night is hard to understand, and a close look proves it to be the Stars and Stripes—which was not even designed until the following summer.

45. "The enemy! The enemy! Turn out!"

46. Later in the war, with the rank of lieutenant colonel, young Washington was to have a brilliant career as a light-horse leader in the South, but he remained, personally, a quiet, diffident man. A fury in the field, who could ride like a centaur and fight like a tiger, he had at one time been destined for the ministry. As for James Monroe, he could sometimes be induced to show the scar in his neck to visitors at the White House when he was fifth President of the United States.

47. *Diary*, pp. 40–41.

48. See article by Marx, in *American Heritage*, Au-

gust, 1955. Also, Knollenberg, *George Washington: The Virginia Period, 1732–1775*, Appendix, Chapter 11.

49. They were kept a few days at Newtown, Pennsylvania, and then were marched to Philadelphia, where they were paraded through the streets just to show the citizens that they were not monsters after all. One of their regimental bands—there had been two at Trenton, for the Germans were believers in martial music—was to play at the first Fourth of July celebration in Philadelphia the following summer. Most of the nonmusicians were scattered through farms in western Pennsylvania and in Virginia, where they were generally liked. "They had been poor soldiers at Trenton; but they made most excellent prisoners." Trevelyan, III, 120.

50. Lawrenceville.

51. Part of the present Jersey City.

52. *History*, I, 177. The italics are his. It should be pointed out, however, that Judge Jones had a grudge against the British, who had never paid him what he thought he ought to get for all that livestock they took from his Long Island farm.

53. It was to be greatly enlarged, to its present size, just after the Napoleonic wars, when the rank of Knight Commander was devised.

54. January 18 was not *really* the Queen's birthday. She had been born in midsummer. But so, unfortunately, had the King; and it would hardly do to have two such important occasions come close together; so the Queen's birthday anniversary was arbitrarily shifted to January 18.

GLOSSARY OF EIGHTEENTH-CENTURY MILITARY TERMS

ABATIS. A roadblock that was made of chopped-down trees piled on top of one another, the branches toward the oncoming or expected enemy.

BARBETTE. A wooden or earthen platform inside of a fortification, on which the cannons were placed in order to allow them to shoot over the rampart.

BASTION. A projecting masonry work, usually V-shaped, on the wall of a fort, outside. From it, attackers along the CURTAIN could be cross-fired.

BLUNDERBUSS. A short chunky weapon, a musket, featured by a huge bell-shaped muzzle. The blunderbuss could discharge a lethal shower of stones, nails, lead slugs, what-have-you—but only for a short distance. Despite the popular picture, it seems certain that none of the Pilgrim Fathers carried blunderbusses. Why should they? The blunderbuss was no good as a bird gun, and any reasonably nimble Indian could hurl his tomahawk ten times the distance that a blunderbuss would carry.

The blunderbuss was good only at close quarters, where its enormous muzzle had a frightening effect. It was favored by the drivers of stage coaches and by householders who had some cause to expect burglars. It was never, properly, a military weapon, though it might sometimes be used, *ad terrorum*, in hit-and-run raids.

BROWN BESS was the nickname of a musket introduced into the British Army in 1682 and which, with minor modifications, continued to be the official arm until 1842. It was, for the time, unexpectedly short and light; and it was efficient. That it was not accurate did not trouble war-makers, who placed all emphasis upon controlled mass fire rather than upon marksmanship. It could be reloaded very quickly. Americans treasured the Brown Bess whenever they could get them from prisoners. The gun had a naturally brown walnut stock, while its barrels and other metal parts had been artificially browned with acid: hence the name.

CANISTER was a canvas or cloth bag filled with small round lead or iron pellets and crammed into a cannon on top of a charge of gunpowder. It would not carry as far as solid shot, but it was deadly at close quarters.

CARCASS. Nothing to do with a cadaver. It was a metal can punched with holes and filled with oiled rags that were set ablaze when the carcass was shot from a cannon. The purpose, of course, was to cause a building or a whole town to catch fire. Carcasses were used from warships in the Battle of Bunker Hill, to destroy the deserted village of Charlestown, which in the beginning had harbored snipers. It was not very effective in that particular brush, and Marines had to be landed with old-fashioned torches to finish the job.

CASE SHOT. Another name for CANISTER.

COHORN was one of the few words in the military vocabulary of the time that was not French. It, and the weapon—a small stubby howitzer—were originally Dutch: *coehoorn*.

Glossary

COUNTERSCARP. The outer wall or slope of the ditch surrounding a fort. The inner wall was the SCARP.

CHEVAUX-DE-FRISE. A crisscross of heavy timbers, usually tipped with steel spikes, calculated to stop infantry. In the Revolution, however, this was used underwater in an effort to prevent ships from passing a certain point.

CURTAIN. The wall of a fortification between BASTION, towers, or other crossfire projections.

DEMILUNES were half-moon-shaped outworks, not large.

EMBRASURE. An opening in a PARAPET through which a cannon is fired.

EPAULEMENT. The "shoulder" of a fort wall; the place where the CURTAIN and BASTION meet.

FASCINES were bundles of twigs and sticks hastily assembled and tied together. They were used for constructing gun platforms and, even more, for filling ditches to permit the passage of military vehicles. From such a bundle, the symbol of ancient Rome, came the name of the late unlamented fascists.

FEU DE JOIE. This was a musket salute performed by two double files, every other man firing the first time, the rest the second time on the way back. It was a complicated business and was not often practiced in the Continental Army, in the beginning because the men were not skilled enough, later because they didn't have the gunpowder to spare, though there was a famous exception at the end of the terrible Valley Forge winter in a ceremony formally greeting the news of the alliance with France.

FLANK COMPANIES. In each British infantry regiment there were a company of grenadiers (who no longer carried grenades) and a company of so-called light infantry, and these were traditionally placed upon the flanks. They were elite troops. When there was an especially dangerous or delicate mission to perform, the flank companies were pulled out of various regiments. This was done, for example, on the 1775 raid on Concord, the scrape that started the Revolution. *All* of those redcoats were flank-company members.

FLÈCHE. A small defensive ditch, unroofed, in the shape of an arrowhead, the point toward the expected enemy. (The word means "arrow" in French.) It was an outwork, a deterrent, a stopgap, not a real fortlet.

GABIONS were baskets made of any material, wicker being preferred, and filled with earth and stones. Clumsy, heavy things, they were used for shoring up parapets, filling ditches, protecting field guns. They were the eighteenth-century equivalent of sandbags.

GRAPE or GRAPESHOT was similar to CANISTER except that the balls were smaller and there were more of them.

HOWITZER meant then exactly what it does today: a smallish cannon sharply uptilted, used, mostly in mountain warfare, to lob shells or balls into a protected position.

MATROSS. A sort of assistant artilleryman who helped to handle a fieldpiece in action. He was a regular member of the army, not like the horse drivers who, in both armies, were hired civilians, and who retired when the guns began to boom—if not sooner.

MORTAR. Just what it is now—a short large-calibered piece of ordnance so trunnioned that it can shoot very high.

PARAPET. The wall of a fortification.

PICKET. A small party of foot soldiers sent forth in advance of the army to feel out the enemy and harass him if he approaches.

POUNDAGE. Field guns, whether on ship or ashore, were rated by the weight of the balls they could fire, which were reckoned

Glossary 167

in pounds avoirdupois. Thus, four-pounder, six-pounder, etc. This applied only to solid ball, not to CANISTER or GRAPE or CARCASSES.

RAMPART. Parapet.

RAVELIN. This was a small earthwork, an outwork, with only two faces, something like a FLÈCHE.

REDAN. It would take an expert to distinguish this from a RAVELIN, though it might be somewhat smaller.

REDOUBT. This was larger and stronger. It might be a square or some other multi-angled shape, but it was always completely enclosed, never open at one end.

SAUCISSON. This, in French, means a large or German-type sausage. In eighteenth-century armies it meant a large FASCINE of roughly that shape.

SPONTOON. This was a sort of halberd or pike carried by sergeants on both sides, for protection purposes, when battle was expected. Often too these were carried by officers, whose toothpicky swords could scarcely be expected to prevail against an infantryman with a six-foot musket *and* bayonet.

TENAILLE. A small, low fortification, sometimes with only one entrance, sometimes with two, occasionally roofed, placed for annoyance purposes outside of the CURTAIN between two BASTIONS.

UP IN THE AIR. An unprotected flank (such as the Continental left on Long Island) was said to have been left "up in the air."

SELECTED BIBLIOGRAPHY

ADAIR, DOUGLASS, see OLIVER, PETER.

ADAMS, CHARLES FRANCIS. *Studies Military and Diplomatic, 1775–1865.* New York: The Macmillan Company, 1911.
———, "The Battle of Long Island," *American Historical Review,* I, 3.
———, see ADAMS, JOHN.

ADAMS, JOHN. *The Works of John Adams, with Life,* edited by Charles Francis Adams, 10 vols. Boston: Little, Brown and Company, 1850–56.

ALDEN, JOHN RICHARD. *General Charles Lee: Traitor or Patriot?* Baton Rouge: Louisiana State University Press, 1951.
———, *The American Revolution, 1775–1783.* New York: Harper & Brothers, 1954.
———, see WARD, CHRISTOPHER.

ANDERSON, TROYER STEELE. *The Command of the Howe Brothers During the American Revolution.* New York and London: Oxford University Press, 1936.

BAKER, WILLIAM SPOHN. *Itinerary of General Washington from June 15, 1775, to December 23, 1783*. Philadelphia: J. B. Lippincott Company, 1892.

BANCROFT, GEORGE. *History of the United States*, 6 vols. Boston: Little, Brown and Company, 1876.

BAUERMEISTER, see UHLENDORF, BERNHARD.

BELCHER, HENRY. *The First American Civil War*, 2 vols. London: The Macmillan Company, 1911.

BELKNAP, DR. JEREMY. *Journal*. (Proceedings of the Massachusetts Historical Society 1858–1860, first series, Vol. IV.)

BILL, ALFRED HOYT. *New Jersey and the Revolutionary War*. Princeton: D. Van Nostrand Company, Inc., 1964.
———, *The Campaign of Princeton, 1776–1777*. Princeton: Princeton University Press, 1948.

BILLIAS, GEORGE ATHAN. *General John Glover and His Marblehead Mariners*. New York: Henry Holt and Company, 1960.

BLIVEN, BRUCE, JR. *Battle for Manhattan*. New York: Henry Holt and Company, 1955.

BLUMENTHAL, WALTER HART. *Women Camp Followers of the American Revolution*. Philadelphia: George S. McManus Company, 1952.

BOLTON, CHARLES KNOWLES. *The Private Soldier Under Washington*. New York: Charles Scribner's Sons, 1902.

BOTTA, CHARLES. *History of the War of the Independence of the United States of America*, 8th ed., 2 vols. Translated from the Italian by George Alexander Otis. New Haven: T. Brainard, 1840.

BREWINGTON, MARION V. "Washington's Boats at the Delaware Crossing," *American Neptune*, II, 167–70.

Selected Bibliography

BROOKS, NOAH. *Henry Knox, a Soldier of the Revolution.* New York: G. P. Putnam's Sons, 1900.

BROWN, WELDON A. *Empire or Independence: A Study in the Failure of Reconciliation, 1774–1783.* Baton Rouge: Louisiana State University Press, 1941.

CALLAHAN, NORTH. *Henry Knox: General Washington's General.* New York: Rinehart and Co., 1958.

CARRINGTON, HENRY B. *Battles of the American Revolution, 1775–1783.* New York, Chicago, and New Orleans: A. S. Barnes and Company, 1876.
———, *Washington the Soldier.* New York: Charles Scribner's Sons, 1899.

CHANNING, EDWARD. *A History of the United States,* 6 vols. New York: The Macmillan Company, 1905–25.

CLARK, DORA MAE. *British Opinion and the American Revolution.* New Haven: Yale University Press, 1930.

COMMAGER, HENRY STEELE, and MORRIS, RICHARD B., editors. *The Spirit of 'Seventy-Six: The Story of the American Revolution as told by Participants,* 2 vols. Indianapolis: The Bobbs-Merrill Company, 1958.

CRESSWELL, NICHOLAS. *Journal.* New York: The Dial Press, 1928.

CURTIS, E. E. *The British Army in the American Revolution.* New Haven: Yale University Press, 1926.

DAVIDSON, PHILIP. *Propaganda and the American Revolution, 1763–1783.* Chapel Hill: University of North Carolina Press, 1941.

DAVIS, GENERAL W. W. H. "Washington on the West Bank of the Delaware, 1776," *The Pennsylvania Magazine of History and Biography,* IV, 2, 133–63.

DAWSON, HENRY BARTON. *Battles of the United States by Sea and Land.* 2 vols. New York: Johnson, Fry and Co., 1853.
———, *Westchester County, New York, in the American Revolution.* Morrisania, N.Y.: 1886. Privately printed.

DE LANCEY, EDWARD F. "Mount Washington and Its Capture, November 16th, 1776," *The Magazine of American History* (1877), I.
———, see JONES, THOMAS.

DRAKE, FRANCIS SAMUEL. *Life and Correspondence of Henry Knox.* Boston: S. G. Drake, 1873.

EELKING, MAX VON. *The German Allied Troops in the North American War of Independence, 1776–1783.* Translated from the German by J. G. Rosengarten. Albany: Joel Munsell's Sons, 1893.

ESPOSITO, COLONEL VINCENT J., editor. *The West Point Atlas of American Wars.* New York: Frederick A. Praeger, 1959.

FIELD, THOMAS W. *The Battle of Long Island.* Brooklyn: The Long Island Historical Society, 1869.

FISHER, SYDNEY GEORGE. *The Struggle for American Independence,* 2 vols. Philadelphia: J. B. Lippincott Company, 1909.

FISKE, JOHN. *The American Revolution,* 2 vols. Boston: Houghton Mifflin and Company, 1897.

FITZPATRICK, JOHN CLEMENT. *George Washington Himself: A Common-Sense Biography Written from His Manuscripts.* Indianapolis: The Bobbs-Merrill Company, 1933.
———, *The Spirit of the Revolution: New Light from Some of the Original Sources of American History.* Boston and New York: Houghton Mifflin Company, 1924.
———, see WASHINGTON, GEORGE.

FORD, PAUL LEICESTER. "Lord Howe's Commission to Pacify the Colonies," *The Atlantic Monthly* (June, 1896), LXXVII, 464.

Selected Bibliography

FORTESCUE, SIR JOHN. *History of the British Army*, 10 vols. New York: The Macmillan Company, 1899–1920.

FREEMAN, DOUGLAS SOUTHALL. *George Washington: A Biography*, 6 vols. New York: Charles Scribner's Sons, 1948–54.

FULLER, J. F. C. *Decisive Battles of the U.S.A.* New York: Thomas Yoseloff, 1942.

GANOE, WILLIAM ADDLEMAN. *The History of the United States Army*, revised edition. New York and London: D. Appleton-Century Company, 1943.

GARDNER, FRANK A. "Colonel John Glover's Marblehead Regiment," *Massachusetts Magazine*, I, 14–20, and 85–102.

GORDON, WILLIAM. *The History of the Rise, Progress, and Establishment of the Independence of the United States of America*, 4 vols. London: Printed for the author, 1788.

GREENE, FRANCIS VINTON. *General Greene.* New York: D. Appleton and Company, 1893.
———, *The Revolutionary War and the Military Policy of the United States.* New York: Charles Scribner's Sons, 1911.

GREENE, GEORGE WASHINGTON. *The Life of Nathanael Greene, Major-General in the Army of the Revolution*, 3 vols. New York: G. P. Putnam and Son, 1876 (Vol. I); Hurd and Houghton, 1871 (vols. II and III).

HALLOWAY, CHARLOTTE MOLYNEUX. *Nathan Hale, the Martyr-Hero of the Revolution.* London and New York: F. Tennyson Neely, 1899.

HAMMOND, OTIS A., editor. *Letters and Papers of Major-General John Sullivan, Continental Army*, 3 vols. Concord: The New Hampshire Historical Society, 1930.

HARTE, CHARLES RUFUS. *The River Obstructions of the Revolutionary War.* Hartford: Connecticut Society of Civil Engineers, 1946.

HATCH, LOUIS CLINTON. *The Administration of the American Revolutionary Army.* New York: Longmans, Green and Co., 1904.

HAVEN, C. C. *Thirty Days in New Jersey Ninety Years Ago.* Trenton: The State Gazette, 1867.

HEATH, WILLIAM. *Memoirs of Major-General Heath.* Boston: I. Thomas and E. T. Andrews, 1798.

HOW, DAVID. *Diary.* Morrisania, N.Y.: privately printed, 1865.

JAMESON, J. FRANKLIN. *The American Revolution Considered as a Social Movement.* Boston: The Beacon Press, 1961.

JOHNSON, HENRY PHELPS. *Nathan Hale 1776: Biography and Memorials.* New Haven: Yale University Press, 1914.
———, *The Battle of Brooklyn Heights.* Brooklyn: The Long Island Historical Society.
———, *The Battle of Harlem Heights, September 16, 1776.* New York: Columbia University Press, 1897.
———, *The Campaign of 1776 Around New York and Brooklyn.* Brooklyn: Long Island Historical Society, 1878.
———, see TALLMADGE, COLONEL BENJAMIN.

JONES, THOMAS. *History of New York During the Revolutionary War,* 2 vols., edited by Edward Floyd De Lancey. New York: The New-York Historical Society, 1879.

KNOLLENBERG, BERNHARD. *Washington and the Revolution: A Reappraisal.* New York: The Macmillan Company, 1940.
———, *George Washington: The Virginia Period, 1732–1775.* Durham, N.C.: Duke University Press, 1964.

LACY, DAN. *The Meaning of the American Revolution.* New York: New American Library, 1964.

LECKY, W. E. H. *History of England in the Eighteenth Century,* 8 vols. London: Longmans, Green and Co., 1878–90.

Selected Bibliography 175

LEFFERTS, CHARLES M. *Uniforms of the American, British, French, and German Armies in the War of the American Revolution, 1775–1783*, edited by Alexander J. Wall. New York: The New-York Historical Society, 1926.

LOSSING, B. L. *Pictorial Field Book of the Revolution*, 2 vols. New York: Harper & Brothers, 1859.

LOWELL, EDWARD J. *The Hessians and Other German Auxiliaries of Great Britain in the Revolutionary War*. New York: Harper & Brothers, 1884.

LUNDIN, LEONARD. *Cockpit of the Revolution: The War for Independence in New Jersey*. Princeton: Princeton University Press, 1940.

MACKENZIE, FREDERICK. *Diary of Frederick Mackenzie*, 2 vols. Cambridge: Harvard University Press, 1930.

MAHAN, ALFRED THAYER. "Admiral Earl Howe," *The Atlantic Monthly* (January, 1894), LXXIII, 435.
———, *The Major Operations of the Navies in the War of American Independence*. London: Sampson Low, Marston and Company, Ltd., 1913.

MARX, RUDOLPH. "A Medical Profile of George Washington," *American Heritage* (August, 1955).

MONTRESOR, see SCULL, G. D.

MONTROSS, LYNN. *Rag, Tag and Bobtail: The Story of the Continental Army*. New York: Harper and Brothers, 1952.

MORGAN, EDMUND S. *The Birth of the Republic, 1763–1789*. Chicago: University of Chicago Press, 1956.

MOORE, FRANK. *Songs and Ballads of the American Revolution*. New York: D. Appleton and Co., 1856.

MOORE, GEORGE H. *The Treason of Charles Lee, Major-General, Second in Command in the American Army of the Revolution*. New York: The New-York Historical Society, 1860.

MORRIS, RICHARD B., see COMMAGER, HENRY STEELE.

NAMIER, LEWIS. *England in the Age of the American Revolution.* London: Macmillan and Company, Ltd., 1930.

OLIVER, PETER. *Origin and Progress of the American Revolution: A Tory View*, edited by Douglass Adair and John A. Schutz. San Marino: The Huntington Library, 1961.

OTIS, GEORGE ALEXANDER, see BOTTA, CHARLES.

PARTRIDGE, BELLAMY. *Sir Billy Howe.* London and New York: Longmans, Green and Co., 1932.

PECKHAM, HOWARD H. *The War for Independence: A Military History.* Chicago: University of Chicago Press, 1958.

PENNYPACKER, MORTON. *General Washington's Spies on Long Island and in New York.* Brooklyn: Long Island Historical Society, 1939.

RICHESON, CHARLES R. *British Politics and the American Revolution.* Norman, Okla.: University of Oklahoma Press, 1954.

ROBSON, ERIC. *The American Revolution in Its Political and Military Aspects, 1763–1783.* London: The Batchworth Press, 1955.

ROSENGARTEN, J. C., see EELKING, MAX VON.

SABINE, LORENZO. *Biographical Sketches of Loyalists of the American Revolution.* 2 vols. Boston: Little, Brown and Co., 1864.

SCHACHNER, NATHAN. *Alexander Hamilton.* New York: D. Appleton-Century Company, 1946.

SCHEER, GEORGE F., and RANKIN, HUGH F. *Rebels and Redcoats.* Cleveland and New York: The World Publishing Company, 1957.

SCHLESINGER, ARTHUR MEIER. "The American Revolution Reconsidered," *Political Science Quarterly*, XXXIV, 61–78.

SCHOULER, JAMES. *Americans of 1776.* New York: Dodd, Mead & Co., 1906.

SCHUTZ, JOHN A., see OLIVER, PETER.

SCHWAB, JOHN C. *The Revolutionary History of Fort Number 8 on Morris Heights, New York City.* New Haven: privately printed, 1897.

SCULL, G. D., editor, *The Montresor Journals.* New York: The New-York Historical Society, 1881.

STEDMAN, CHARLES. *The History of the Origin, Progress, and Termination of the American War*, 2 vols. London: printed for the author, 1794.

STEELE, MATTHEW F. *American Campaigns*, 2 vols. Washington: Byron S. Adams, 1909.

STRYKER, WILLIAM S. *The Battles of Trenton and Princeton.* Boston: Houghton Mifflin and Company, 1898.
——— "The Princeton Surprise, 1777," *The Magazine of American History*, VIII, 1, 1882.

STUART, I. W. *Life of Captain Nathan Hale, the Martyr-Hero of the Revolution.* Hartford, Conn.: F. A. Brown, 1856.

TALLMADGE, COLONEL BENJAMIN. *Memoir*, edited by Henry Phelps Johnston. New York: The Gilliss Press, 1904.

THACHER, JAMES. *Military Journal of the American Revolution.* Hartford, Conn.: Hurlbut, Williams & Co., 1862.

TREVELYAN, GEORGE OTTO. *The American Revolution*, 6 vols. Longmans, Green, and Co., 1905.

TYLER, MOSES COIT. *The Literary History of the American Revolution*, 2 vols. New York: G. P. Putnam's Sons, 1897.
——— "The Party of the Loyalists in the American Revolution," *American Historical Review* (October, 1895), I, i.

UHLENDORF, BERNHARD A., editor. *Revolution in America: Confidential Letters and Journals, 1776–1784, of Adjutant General Major Bauermeister of the Hessian Forces.* New Brunswick, N.J.: Rutgers University Press, 1957.

VAN DOREN, CARL. *Benjamin Franklin.* New York: The Viking Press, 1938.

VAN TYNE, CLAUDE HALSTEAD. *The Loyalists in the American Revolution.* New York: Peter Smith, 1929.
——— *The War of Independence: American Phase.* Boston and New York: Houghton Mifflin Company, 1929.

WALL, ALEXANDER J. see LEFFERTS, CHARLES M.

WALLACE, WILLARD M. *Appeal to Arms: A Military History of the American Revolution.* New York: Harper & Brothers, 1951.

WARD, CHRISTOPHER. *The War of the Revolution,* 2 vols., edited by John Richard Alden. New York: The Macmillan Company, 1952.

WASHINGTON, GEORGE. *The Writings of George Washington, from the Original Manuscript Sources, 1745–1799,* edited by John Clement Fitzpatrick, 39 vols. Washington: U.S. Government Printing Office, 1931–1944.

WELLER, JAC. "Guns of Destiny: Field Artillery in the Trenton-Princeton Campaign," *Military Affairs* (Spring, 1956), XX.

WERTENBAKER, THOMAS JEFFERSON. *The Battle of Princeton.* Princeton: The Princeton Battle Monument, 1922.

WILD, EBENEZER. *Journal, 1776–1781.* (Proceedings of the Massachusetts Historical Society, second series, Vol. VI, October 1890.)

Index

A
Adams, Abigail, 6
Adams, John, 6, 46, 47, 49; notes 10, 11
Anderson, Richard, 121
Anne, Queen of England, 10
Arnold, Benedict, 5
Altenbockum, Capt. von, 124

B
Barré, Col. Isaac, 2
Barton, Col., 46
Belknap, Jeremy, 1
Blackler, William, 118
Browne, Mountfort, 89
Bunker Hill, Battle of, 3, 11, 40, 41; notes 4, 9
Burgoyne, Gen. John, 3, 98
Burr, Aaron, 59, 60

C
Cadwalader, Col. John, 109, 121, 131–4, 141–2
Catherine of Russia, 4, 28
Clinton, Maj. Gen. Henry, 3, 8, 18, 23, 90, 149
Cornwallis, Gen. Lord, 23, 82, 83, 89, 90–2, 97–8, 105, 137–138, 140–1, 144, 148–9
Covenhoven, John, 89
Cresswell, Nicholas, 147

D
Dechow, Maj., 105, 127
Declaration of Independence, 13, 89
Dickinson, Philemon, 124
Donop, Col. von, 92, 105, 109, 118, 120, 126, 130, 132–4, 148
Douglas, Capt. William, 53, 66
Durham, Robert, 113

E
Erskine, Sir William, 138
Ewing, Brig. Gen. James, 109, 111, 112, 126, 131

F
Fermoy, Brig. Gen. Matthias Alexis Roche de, 108, 126, 137
Fitzgerald, Lt., 143
Fleming, Capt. John, 142
Forrest, Capt. Thomas, 137
Franklin, Benjamin, 16, 47, 48
Frederick the Great, 28, 29

G

Gage, Lt. Gen. Thomas, 3
Gates, Maj. Gen. Horatio, 94, 99, 102, 109, 110-2, 131; note 41
George I, King of England, 10
George III, King of England, 14, 44, 46, 48, 49, 86-7, 101, 149, 150
Germain, Lord George, 103-4
Glover, Col. John, 42, 46, 72, 108, 110, 112, 135
Grant, Maj. Gen. Sir James, 31-4, 36-7, 130, 134, 148
Greene, Maj. Gen. Nathanael, 25-6, 46, 51, 70, 77-9, 83, 108, 110, 116, 119, 120-1, 126

H

Hale, Nathan, 63, 68, 70
Hamilton, Alexander, 59, 60, 125, 127
Hancock, John, 3, 51
Hand, Col. Edward, 137
Harcourt, Lt. Col. William, 98-101
Harlem Heights, Battle of, 63-7
Haslet, Col. John, 27, 73, 75, 116, 142
Hausegger, Col., 137
Heath, Maj. Gen. William, 42, 78, 93
Heister, Gen. von, 23, 34, 37
Honeyman, John, 106-8
How, David, 129
Howe, George Augustus, Viscount, 11
Howe, Richard, Viscount
 origin, 10, 11

Howe, Richard (*cont.*)
 as peace commissioner, 14, 16, 46-9, 50
 as admiral, 17-9, 32, 36, 43, 86-7, 89, 102-4; note 6
Howe, Maj. Gen. William, 3, 9, 10
 as peace commissioner, 14, 16, 17, 46, 47, 49, 50
 as general, 19, 21, 23, 27, 33, 41, 43-5, 52, 60-2, 68, 70-73, 75-9, 82, 86-9, 90, 102-104, 146, 149, 150
Humpton, Col. Richard, 91
Hunt, Abraham, 118
Hutchinson, Col., 42

J

Jones, Judge John, 149; note 52

K

Keith, William, 108
Kielmannsegge, Baroness von, 10, 11
Knowlton, Capt. Thomas, 63-6
Knox, Brig. Gen. Henry, 8, 16-17, 46, 108, 116, 135, 139

L

Lee, Maj. Gen. Charles, 1-9, 19, 59, 63, 70, 72, 78, 89, 90, 93, 94, 97-9, 100-2; notes 33, 36
Leitch, Maj. Andrew, 65-6
Leslie, Maj. Gen. Alexander, 130, 134, 140
Leutze, Emanuel, note 44

Long Island, Battle of, 20–44, 51
Loring, Joshua, 76, 82–3
Loring, Mrs. Joshua, 76, 82; note 27

M

Macwhorter, Rev. Alexander, 109
Magaw, Col. Robert, 77, 79, 80
Mawhood, Lt. Col. Charles, 140, 141, 143
Mercer, Maj. Gen. Hugh, 42, 46, 79, 108, 116, 123, 125–126, 141–2.
Mifflin, Maj. Gen. Thomas, 135
Monroe, James, 127–8; note 46
Montgomery, Maj. Gen. Richard, 5
Moore, Benjamin, 119
Moultrie, Brig. Gen. William, 18–9
Murray, Robert, 57
Murray, Mrs. Robert, 61; note 19

P

Paine, Thomas, 95
Parker, Sir Peter, 18, 19
Paterson, Lt. Col., 17
Percy, Lord, 23, 71, 78
Piel, Lt. Jacob, 125
Potts, Stacy, 118
Prescott, Brig. Gen. Richard, 89
Princeton, Battle of, 139–145
Putnam, Maj. Gen. Israel, 23, 26, 31, 46, 56–7, 59, 60–1, 63, 69, 79, 96, 109, 111
Putnam, Col. Rufus, 79

R

Rall, Col. Johann Gottlieb von, 105, 118, 120, 124, 125, 148
Reed, Col. Joseph, 16, 94, 140
Rutledge, Edward, 47

S

Sackville, Lord George, *see* Germain
St. Clair, Brig. Gen. Arthur, 108
Sargent, Col., 108
Schulenberg, Baroness von, 10
Scott, Col. Charles, 137
Seymour, Commodore Thomas, 104, 137
Smallwood, Col. Alexander, 27, 75
Stanislaus, King, 4
Stansbury, Joseph, 97
Stark, Col. John, 108
Stephen, Brig Gen. Adam, 108, 116, 121–3
Stirling, Maj. Gen. Alexander Lord, 31–2, 37, 46, 89, 90, 108, 116, 126–7
Stockton, Richard, 89
Sullivan, Maj. Gen. John, 23, 26, 34–7, 46, 89, 98, 102, 108, 110, 118, 119, 120, 124

T

Trenton, Battle of, 121–138
Tucker, Judge Samuel, 89

W

Ward, Maj. Gen. Artemas, 3
Washington, George, 3, 4, 5, 6, 8, 9, 13, 16–7, 55–6, 62, 77–9, 80, 83, 89, 90–4, 97,

Washington, George (*cont.*)
102–4, 106–7, 109–112, 115, 118–9, 146–7; notes 23, 33
at Long Island, 22, 25–6, 37, 42–4, 51–2
at Harlem Heights, 63–5, 67
at White Plains, 72–3, 75
at Trenton, 121–2, 128–9, 130, 133–4
at Princeton, 142–4
Washington, Capt. William, 127–8; note 46

Weymouth, Viscount, 150
Wheedon, Brig. Gen. George, 46, 127
White Plains, Battle of, 73–5
White, Widow, 98–9, 100, 102
Wiederhold, Lt. Andreas, 123
Wilkes, John, 2
Wilkinson, James, 111; note 43
Wolfe, Gen. James, 108

Y

Yeates, Lt. Bartholomew, 142

www.ingramcontent.com/pod-product-compliance
Lightning Source LLC
LaVergne TN
LVHW041620070426
835507LV00008B/350